CONTRIB

K. B. Nowlan, Lecturer in Mo... sity College, Dublin

Terence de Vere White, Literary Editor of *Irish Times,* author

T. Desmond Williams, Professor of Modern History, U.C.D.

David Thornley, Lecturer in Political Science, Trinity College, Dublin

James Meenan, Professor of Political Economy and National Economics, U.C.D.

F. S. L. Lyons, Professor of Modern History, University of Kent

T. Barrington, Director, Institute of Public Administration

Rev. Sean O Cathain, S.J., Lecturer in Education, U.C.D.

Francis MacManus, Director of Talks, Radio Eireann

Nicholas Mansergh, Professor, St. John's College, Cambridge

David Kennedy, Professor of History, St. Malachy's College, Belfast

J. L. McCracken, Professor of History, Magee University College

Vincent Grogan, S.C.

Donal Nevin, Research Officer, Irish Congress of Trade Unions

The Years of the Great Test

EDITED BY

FRANCIS MacMANUS

THE MERCIER PRESS

4 BRIDGE ST., CORK

Published for Radio-Telefis Eireann by The Mercier Press, 1967

INTRODUCTION

Every autumn, winter, and spring since September 1953, Radio Telefis Eireann has been broadcasting half-hour lectures, named in honour of Thomas Davis. Inspired by one of his famous sayings, 'Educate that you may be free,' the aim of these lectures has been to provide in popular form what is best in Irish scholarship and the sciences.

Most of the lectures have been in series ; many have been single broadcasts ; some have been in English, some in Irish. In the comparatively short time that has passed since they were initiated the lectures have dealt with many aspects and with many centuries of Irish social life, history, science and literature. The lecturers, distinguished for their special learning at home and abroad, have been drawn from many nations but mainly from Ireland.

The general titles of some of the series provide an idea of the variety and scope of the lectures: *The Celts* ; *The Integrity of Yeats* ; *The Irish at War* ; *The Yeats We Knew* ; *Leaders and Workers* and *Early Irish Poetry*.

The talks included here were delivered in 1962.

CONTENTS

PRESIDENT COSGRAVE'S LAST ADMINISTRATION

Kevin B. Nowlan

A little after midnight on 11th August 1927, an official statement was issued by the Fianna Fail party. It declared that the Fianna Fail deputies had met and resolved to present themselves at 'the Clerk's Office of the Free State Dail' 'for the purpose of complying with the provisions of Article 17 of the Constitution by inscribing their names in the book kept for the purpose... But so that there may be no doubt as to their attitude... the Fianna Fail deputies hereby give public notice... that they purpose to regard the declaration as an empty formality and repeat that their only allegiance is to the Irish Nation'. The 'empty formality' was the controversial Oath of Allegiance contained in the 1922 Constitution of Saorstát Éireann. With that historic decision to subscribe to the 'empty formality', a dangerous crisis was ended; a crisis which, had it not been speedily resolved, might well have imperilled the whole future of democratic, parliamentary government in Ireland.

By the year 1925-6, the republicans, refusing to have any share in the post-Treaty system, and clinging to the defiant claim that the Second Dail was the only legitimate government, were clearly on the losing side. They had been defeated in the Civil War, the instruments of effective government were all in the hands of the pro-Treaty party and they were divided among themselves. In 1925, for example, the I.R.A. had decided to reassert its autonomy and, in effect, withdraw from the jurisdiction of the now very shadowy civil government of the Republic.

The Irish Free State was working, it was internationally recognised and its laws were being enforced. And though the Republicans were still a very important factor in Irish politics, the question had sometime to be asked: could they afford to remain indefinitely in the wilderness? The use of force, since the Civil War, was becoming less and less practicable and military and financial resources were very limited. The verdict of the electorate, in favour of peace and order, could not be completely ignored and the Free State's administrators were strong and able men. Mr. de Valera asked that question and the result was a major split in the Sinn Fein movement and the emergence of Fianna Fail, in the early summer of 1926, as an independent republican organisation under de Valera's leadership. From the beginning, Fianna Fail sought to unite certain essentially political, almost symbolic, claims with the persistent demand for a very positive, self-sufficient economic policy – a potent combination especially in the difficult years of 1931 and 1932.

Mr. de Valera withdrew from Sinn Fein, because he failed to secure from that movement a clear mandate for a new policy which he believed would rescue the republicans from their dangerous isolation. In March 1926, he asked Sinn Fein, of which he was President, to accept the proposition that 'once the admission oaths of the Twenty Six and Six County assemblies are removed, it becomes a question not of principle but of policy whether or not republican representatives should attend these assemblies'. And he further proposed that candidates should be put forward at the next Free State general election who would 'assert their right to enter any assembly where the other elected representatives meet for public business'. These proposals sum up in its essentials the policy de Valera was to elaborate in the new Fianna Fail Party in 1926 and 1927. He stressed that while the Free State Dail was not the legitimate parliament of the republic, he was prepared to use it to achieve full independence, provided he and his followers did not have to take the Oath of Allegiance. As Mr. Sean Lemass put it, with characteristic vigour, in February 1927, they would assert their right to represent their constituents in the Dail 'without being forced to take an oath repugnant to them and to all decent Irishmen'.

Fianna Fail spokesmen, however, were careful to stress their patience. Even if they did not win a clear majority at the coming elections they were confident of their ultimate success. If the Oath remained to bar their entry into the

8

Dail, then they would strive to induce a majority of the people's representatives to meet elsewhere, outside the Dail and presumably take over the administration of the country. De Valera was careful not to rule out the possibility of force being used as a legitimate weapon to achieve national ends, but, as he told the first Fianna Fail Ard Fheis, 'a nation within itself ought to be able to settle its policy so that all occasions of civil conflict between its members might be obviated'. Peaceful methods, patience, public support and even legal arguments would ultimately carry the day. But what would happen, if for example, a law were passed aimed at excluding from the Free State elections all candidates who refused to sign an undertaking to the effect that they would accept the Oath of Allegiance and take their seats in parliament if elected? The Fianna Fail movement was suddenly presented with this challenge to their whole programme of fighting elections but refusing to take the Oath, in the summer of 1927.

The Dail which was dissolved in May 1927 had been elected in 1923. It was an assembly in which the Cumann na nGaedheal Party, led by Mr. W.T. Cosgrave, commanded a majority among those deputies who sat in the House and who had taken the Oath of Allegiance. This last proviso is an important one, because out of the 153 members entitled to sit, 46 were absentee republican deputies. Should, at any time, all or even a section of the abstentionists take their seats, then clearly the existing balance in Irish parliamentary politics would be seriously upset, if only because the margin between the Cumann na nGaedheal strength and that of the republicans was narrow enough: 57 seats as against the republicans 46. The advent of Fianna Fail, which rapidly supplanted Sinn Fein, brought the day near when that balance would be upset; nearer perhaps than many people realised in the spring of 1927.

There were two general elections in 1927, in June and September, separated by the murder of Kevin O'Higgins, 'a murder stark and hideous' as a Fianna Fail journal described it. The death of O'Higgins, the Vice-President of the Executive Council, was a terrible reminder of how close Ireland still was to the violence of the Civil War, and it was to bring with it the makings of a serious political crisis.

The political scene, even before the murder of O'Higgins was not particularly encouraging. The June elections had proved unsatisfactory, leaving many questions unanswered. The results suggested that Free State politics might well breed a multiplicity of sectional parties, accepting the Treaty with varying degrees of enthusiasm but agreeing on little else. There was even the possibility that the discontented licensed traders would organise a party of their own. The reason for this trend towards sectional parties, in 1927, lay in the nature of the opposition to the Government party in the Dail between 1923 and 1927. Too little credit, I believe, has been given to Tom Johnson and the 15 or so Labour deputies who formed the only effective opposition in Dail Eireann during those years. But the pressure they could exercise was limited and they were moderate non-revolutionary men with little of James Connolly's radicalism about them. In the circumstances, dissatisfaction with specific aspects of the Government's policy, tended to express itself in the formation of groups reflecting special interests rather than comprehensive national policies. Cumann na nGaedheal regarded this development among the pro-Treaty elements with no enthusiasm but they could do little to defeat it.

In one way the intervention of the Fianna Fail Party, in the June election, eased the situation somewhat; the marginal Clann Eireann disappeared. But far more serious than the proliferation of small parties was the uncomfortable fact that the Cosgrave administration lost its overall majority even among those deputies who accepted the Oath, and that at a time when de Valera's new party had won 44 seats at the polls. The inadequacies of Proportional Representation were deplored, but the most pressing question was: what would Mr. de Valera now do?

He was not long in letting his opponents know. He had fought the election on the policy of going into the Dail, provided he would not have to take the Oath. He claimed, when the election results were known that 'if a referendum were held... if the single issue of the oath were put before the people, this infamous penal legislation would be repudiated by an indignant nation'. The Fianna Fail deputies were going to claim their seats in the Dail knowing that the people would 'not tolerate' their being excluded because of the Oath. Mr. de Valera's statement was quickly followed up by a Fianna Fail advertisement claiming that there was no legal authority to exclude any member from the Dail before the Ceann Comhairle was duly elected. It was further claimed that even the Treaty did not make the Oath compulsory. Then on 23rd June, 1927, the day on which the new Dail met, came the dramatic moment when the Fianna Fail deputies sought admission to the Dail Chamber but learned that they would not be admitted unless they subscribed to the Oath. Legal proceedings were instituted in the High Court to test the validity of the exclusion, and Mr. de Valera announced that the necessary 75,000 signatures would be collected to demand a referendum on the Oath question in accordance with the terms of the Constitution.

In the House, from which the Fianna Fail deputies were excluded, Cosgrave was elected President of the Executive Council once more. But the atmosphere was strained, the Labour party was critical of the Government and so was Captain Redmond at the head of his new National League. But the uncertainty of June was soon to be succeeded by horror and anger when Kevin O'Higgins was assassinated.

O'Higgins had been one of the most impressive indeed formidable members of the Cosgrave administration and though all sections of the republican movement repudiated responsibility for the crime, the Government saw in his death a serious challenge to its authority. They replied by introducing three bills which underlined only too clearly the sense of insecurity that still survived in the new Irish state. The first was a Public Safety Bill giving the authorities wide powers to deal with illegal organisations. The other two were constitutional measures aimed at the absentee Fianna Fail deputies. One bill required all candidates at future elections to make a declaration, under oath, that

11

they would take the Oath of Allegiance and sit in the Dail, if elected. The other measure was primarily devised to prevent any attempt by the Fianna Fail party to press for a referendum on the Oath without first taking their seats in the Dail.

The new legislation encountered strong opposition from the Labour deputies, and, before the end of July, de Valera let it be known that if an alternative Government could be formed, and if Fianna Fail could enter the Dail without taking the Oath, they would not press unduly any other issues involving the Treaty during the life-time of that Dail. There was, however, little likelihood of a new Government being formed so long as Fianna Fail remained outside the House. The deadlock was broken when the Fianna Fail deputies, on August 11 subscribed to the 'empty formality' and took their seats.

In coming into Dail Eireann, Mr. de Valera stressed they had acted under duress. Free State legislation had faced them with the alternative of acting as they did or of abandoning all they had achieved; a new civil war would have been 'unpardonable'. 'I grant', he said, 'that what we did was contrary to all our former actions... It was a step painful and humiliating for us who had to take it... There was and is no change of attitude on our part as to the national significance of that Oath'.

We can now see that the Fianna Fail decision was one which, in the long term, gave a new strength and reality to Irish parliamentary life. At the time there was less certainty about the outcome. Men were brought into the Dail, who were pledged to dismantle the Constitution of the Irish Free Sate, to clear the way for a Republican order. And yet the interesting question arises; to what extent may the decision to force Fianna Fail to make a choice represent something more than an emergency measure? Did Cosgrave and his ministers see in the entry of Fianna Fail a possible guarantee of future stability, even if it brought risks for themselves? The other question which the events of 1927 suggest is why did not the abstentionists come into the Dail many years before? Perhaps the best answer to this question lies in the outcome of the Civil War:

the victory of the Pro-Treaty party. There had always been a welcome element of realism in Irish political history. The time for effective protests outside the Dail had passed.

The first result of the entry of Fianna Fail was quickly revealed. Though there was no real fellowship between Fianna Fail, the National League and Labour except a common hostility to the Government, it was sufficient to present Mr. Cosgrave with a fresh challenge. There was much speculation on the possibility of a Labour-Redmond-ite coalition, strange as it might seem, with an indulgent Fianna Fail in the background. The negotiations were rather fruitless, but what did result was a direct vote of no confidence in the Government – which was only saved by the Ceann Comhairle's casting vote and the opportune absence of Ald. Jinks of Sligo. Cumann na nGaedheal was saved from the humiliation of defeat but a fresh general election could hardly have been avoided. And the autumn polls returned the Dail which was to survive until January 1932.

The autumn elections had at least one important result. They helped to destroy the hopes of the minor groups of an independent existence. In contrast, both Cumann na nGaedheal and Fianna Fail gained seats, the one winning 61 the other 57. Cosgrave was again in a minority in the House but backed by the Farmers, what remained of the National League and enough independents he could sur-vive the voting power of Fianna Fail and a much reduced Labour Party. But the era of clear predominance was gone. Opposite him was a solid body of Fianna Fail dep-uties and however, much they may have criticised the Free State and its institutions, their ambition was to form the next administration and, supported by a majority of the people, prepare the way for the full restoration of the Republic.

That autumn of 1927 was a time of decisive importance in the history of the Irish State. The activities of the mili-tant republicans, who rejected de Valera's leadership, would remain of considerable political significance. But neither the I.R.A. nor Saor Eire was destined to wrest political leadership from the parliamentarians, be they the supporters of William Cosgrave or Eamon de Valera.

Throughout our period, the Cumann na nGaedheal Party, maintained a rather fixed political course, which could easily give the impression of an unbending rigidity, a too ready acceptance of the conventional, especially in relation to economic policy and social reform. It is, however, necessary to examine the actions of that Government more closely, since behind that conservatism certain forces of change were operating. Its critics might condemn it for forgetting its Sinn Fein origins, for becoming too committed to the forms and trappings of Empire. But we know that the work done by Mr. McGilligan and the Irish delegations between the Imperial Conference of 1926 and the year 1931, did much to make the Commonwealth the association of sovereign states that it is to-day. Even more important in the Irish context, the events between 1926 and the passage of the Statute of Westminster, made easier, some might say made possible, many of the constitutional changes which followed in the years after 1932.

Again, in the economic field, it would be a gross simplification to describe the Cosgrave administration as merely a free trade one. There were, of course, powerful free trade, or near free trade elements in the Cumann na nGaedheal party, but there were also the friends of moderate protection. I think it fairer to say that as the time of difficulty, in 1930-32, closed in on the Government, the voice of protection became stronger, as witness the decision to put the rather lethargic Tariff Commission on a full-time basis. And yet the impression of conservatism remains. The land legislation is easily forgotten about while the reduction in the Old Age Pension is remembered.

Fianna Fail, from 1927 onwards, was able to attack the Government along a broad front, at a time when the viability of the political and economic basis of post-war Europe was being brought increasingly into doubt. The Government presented the Dail with sound, unexciting budgets year after year; no small achievement when the material destruction and loss of the civil war period is remembered. National loans had been successfully floated, the Shannon Scheme was completed and, by 1931, some useful tariffs had been imposed. But, despite these achievements, the Government's programme lacked the variety and challenge of what Fianna Fail was advocating. As Mr. Cosgrave once ruefully said 'It was one of the privileges of the Opposition that they should table the most attractive and costly programme, and it was one of the disadvantages of the Government that they must provide the means, or answer for non-providing the means'.

Constitutional reform, the removal of the Oath so that all republicans could feel free to enter the Dail, the abolition or thorough reform of the Seanad, a step by step advance to the Republic – these represented one aspect of the Fianna Fail opposition to the Cosgrave administration. And it was combined with a rather subtle attitude to the Dail as an institution. It was still the Free State assembly, not the Republican Dail. In a remarkable speech, in the Dail, in 1929, Mr. de Valera put this point of view as follows: 'You have secured a de facto position... There must be some body in charge to keep order in the community... You have not come by that position legitimately. You brought off a coup d'etat in the summer of 1922'. As a consequence of this, he argued that those republicans who did not follow him into the Dail but continued in the 'organisation' he had left, 'can claim exactly the same continuity that we claimed up to 1925'.

It was not surprising, therefore, that Fianna Fail marched in the same republican parades to Bodenstown as the I.R.A. and Sinn Fein, that critical voices were raised, in 1929, against political arrests and that in 1931, Mr. de Valera could speak with sympathy of the men 'animated with honest motives' who were thrown back on the use of force because they were still unwilling to ignore the Oath and come into the Dail. There were, however, limits to the extent of co-operation between Fianna Fail and the more radical republicans. When, for example, the I.R.A Army Council, in 1927, in an effort to restore republican unity, proposed a common abstentionist front with other republican bodies, Fianna Fail, at once, rejected the idea. Again, Fianna Fail came to lay much emphasis on the de facto authority of the Free State. 'If there is no authority in this House to rule, then there is no authority in any part of the country to rule' as Mr. de Valera expressed it in October 1931. This dual role of Fianna Fail had its obvious advantages, especially in terms of support at election time. It could fulfill its part as a constitutional opposition and yet be counted in the camp of political dissent.

To concentrate on constitutional issues alone would be to put the political events of our period into a false perspective; economic and social issues became of critical importance from 1930 onwards. In contrast to the Government, Fianna Fail came to the economic problems of the time deeply committed to industrial and agricultural self-sufficiency. By 1930-31, tillage and industrialisation became, as it were, the promise of a new Ireland with better social services, and better able to offer practical inducements to the northern counties to come into an independent Irish State.

Protection was a strong political argument in many lands in the years of the Great Depression. The Cosgrave Government now found it necessary to think more urgently in terms of increased protection, but there was no whole-hearted acceptance of a policy of high tariffs. Opinion, on the tariff issue remained divided in government circles, and this weakened the impact of the party on the electorate at a time of considerable economic strain. The Government had other troubles too. Early in 1931, it was defeated, in the Dail, on an old age pensions measure; there was the persistent unemployment problem and a great deal of controversy about agricultural de-rating. Most serious of all, the republican extremists, from 1929 onwards became a source of much concern in Merrion Street.

The late nineteen-twenties and early nineteen-thirties witnessed the growth of extreme right-wing and left-wing movements in Europe. It would have been surprising had Ireland remained completely immune. The Saor Eire organisation, with influential backing in I.R.A. and radical labour circles, was established in 1931. Its programme was boldly socialist; to create 'an independent revolutionary leadership for the working class and working farmers

16

towards the overthrow in Ireland of British imperialism and its ally, Irish capitalism'. Saor Eire was not the only symptom of the new unrest in 1931. There were a number of serious shooting incidents, reports of drilling and evidence of discontent among the small farmers in some areas, and the republican press claimed that the Dublin Brigade of the I.R.A. could muster 2,000 men.

Throughout this period of rapid change, Fianna Fail maintained its dual character – of being both constitutional and republican. Members of the Party again marched with other republicans to Bodenstown in 1931. And though Fianna Fail spokesmen emphasised the *de facto* authority of the Free State, they did not disguise their sense of fellowship with those republicans who refused to come into the Dail. Again, when, in October 1931, the Government rushed through the Oireachtas the rather draconian Constitutional Amendment Bill, to set up the Military Tribunal to try political offences, the Fianna Fail deputies criticised the Bill as excessive and unnecessarily alarmist. But whatever may have been the actual strength of the revolutionary elements, one thing was clear, a general election could not be long delayed.

The Cosgrave Government fought the general election of February 1932 on the basis of its service in the past, its record of firm measures against extremists and the economies it had achieved rather than in terms of a new programme. In contrast to the austerity of the Government's case, Fianna Fail emphasised economic self-sufficiency, the republican ideal and its aspirations to reconcile all sections of national opinion. Not surprisingly, Fianna Fail, with 72 seats was returned as the largest party in the new Dail. It had still to win an absolute majority, but the long era of the Cosgrave administration had ended. If it went out on a certain note of anti-climax, it is well to remember its considerable achievements. Under the unobtrusive but firm leadership of W.T. Cosgrave, the state's administration and financial system were rebuilt out of the chaos left by the war of independence and the civil war, order was restored and the international status of the Irish Free State had been firmly established. When the moment of change came, though some men were fearful for the future stability of the state, William Cosgrave made way, as a good parliamentarian and a good democrat, for the leader of the new government, Mr. Eamon De Valera.

SOCIAL LIFE IN IRELAND 1927–1937

Terence de Vere White

1927 was a significant year in the history of the five year old Irish Free State. The Shannon Scheme (Mr McGilligan's White Elephant as an ebullient critic called it even four years later) was launched. It was the year in which Kevin O'Higgins was assassinated; in which Mr de Valera led his followers into the Dail; in which Mr Jinks, simply by staying away, prolonged the life of Mr Cosgrave's Government. It was the year when the Department of Posts and Telegraphs announced the coming of a national broadcasting service, when public houses were forced to close from three until five o'clock on week-day afternoons, when greyhound racing, not without opposition, was started in Harold's Cross and Mr Timothy Michael Healy, first Governor General, handed the key of the Viceregal Lodge to Mr James McNeill.

To social realist and puritan alike, it may not seem obvious that the condition of the new State called for any restoration of the former glories of the Viceregal régime, glories that the coming of the Aberdeens with their Home Rule principle, good deeds and rigid economies had reduced to the homely atmosphere of the manse after the conspicuous extravagance of Dudleys and Cadogans. And Dublin, ever since the Union, from being one of the brightest capitals of Europe had degenerated into the dreariness of a provincial city.

The arrival of a diplomatic corps in Dublin had begun to lend it a more cosmopolitan air. Our ministers of State had led such strenuous lives that they had had little time for society; but some of them had young wives, and as the country, after Civil War, seemed to have settled down at last, it was to be expected that they should play a prominent part in the social life of the City.

Trinity College had passed through an Athenian phase.

No longer was there a Mahaffy to preside over Georgian societies, dominate the councils of the National Gallery, Royal Irish Academy and Royal Dublin Society, lay down the law on every subject and recall his personal contacts with the crowned heads of Europe. No longer was the education of the country under the sole control of Mr Commissioner Starkie, Fellow of Trinity College, no longer was the Bench and the front row at the Bar the perquisite of Trinity men. Mr Cosgrave's cabinet contained graduates and members of the staff of University College, Dublin, then less than twenty years old.

As for the former Protestant ascendancy, Arthur Griffith and Michael Collins had made overtures to them. Mr Cosgrave had also encouraged them to take part in building the nation and had nominated a generous number for the first Senate. The experience of the Civil War had discouraged some of these and had not added to the number who were prepared to set old loyalties aside to the extent of lending their support to government. The ex-unionists in the country continued to lead their old life – income tax was three shillings in the pound and servants could be had in plenty for less than a pound a week's wages. County kept to itself and its contact with Dublin was the Kildare Street Club and the shows at Ballsbridge. To bridge the gap between this Ireland of Somerville and Ross and the new Ireland was one of the tasks the McNeills attempted and, to outward appearances, achieved.

The melting of the hard core of old ascendancy in Dublin required a less diplomatic, a more practical procedure. The Castle Catholic was the type that most deeply deplored the passing of the Raj. It was all dressed up and now had nowhere to go. The survivor of Protestant ascendancy, unlike his sporting co-religionists in the country, was a quiet living and industrious fellow. It was not by such as he that Dublin won its title, the City of Dreadful Knights. He was principally concerned with the material welfare of his family and the safeguarding of his livelihood. In 1927 he was still firmly entrenched in the banking, commercial, and legal life of Dublin. Perusal of a Dublin directory at the commercial section for any of the years under survey suggests that no change had taken place in Irish life since 1914. The ex-unionist lived as formerly, kept up his club membership – Brian Inglis has given an account of one of his golf-clubs – did not try to identify himself with the country, and his wife, who had servants then, played a great deal of afternoon bridge. If some sent their sons to St Columba's or Portora, many preferred an English public school, not always one of the top ones. Catholics, of the same class, at this time, sent their boys – to Downside, Ampleforth, Beaumont and Stoneyhurst. When I entered Trinity College in 1927, a frequent subject of debate was that Irish boys should go to Irish schools.

The post-treaty climate proved too much for the Sackville Street Club whose members distributed themselves between the Kildare Street and University Clubs. The latter, as it drew on Trinity graduates for its members, was least affected by the change. The impact on Kildare Street Club was more gradual than the blow received by the United Services Club when the military establishment upon which it chiefly depended as a source for members left the country. The Stephen's Green Club cannot have been much ruffled. Founded, like the National Bank by Daniel O'Connell, when Catholics after emancipation found themselves in a social vacuum, it could expect to play a part in the political emancipation that had more recently taken place. In Dún Laoghaire, like the three bears, the Kingstown Yacht Clubs did not all adapt too readily their canvas to the prevailing wind.

The photographs in the press of this period may give a misleading impression that the Irish peers and the landed gentry had gone to ground in 1927 to emerge from their hiding place during the next decade. Their comparative scarcity can be attributed to the slaughter of a generation in the 1914-18 war. Its heirs were still at school or university in the 'twenties. Lords Rosse and Killanin, both of whom were later prominent in Irish life, are only two of many of these. Lord Longford, who was some years older, was already very much a part of the Dublin scene. His father had been killed at the very beginning of that war.

Lord and Lady Longford appear among the guests at the Costume Ball given in Civic Week when Mr Murphy, chairman of the Commissioners who then administered the affairs of the city, acted as host. There had been a military tattoo at Lansdowne Road which 20,000 had attended. Underneath a photograph in the *Irish Tatler and Sketch* of one of the groups present at the ball the caption reads: 'Mrs James McNeill as Betsy Gray, 1798; Queen Maeve, Mrs. Hugh Kennedy; Celtic Chieftain, Mr Donal O'Sullivan; Augustus Caesar, Senator Oliver St John Gogarty; a Norman lady, Miss Hackett; Lord Longford as his own grandfather; seventeenth century French Costume, Marchioness MacSwiney; Mounted Grattan Volunteer, Major B. O'Brien; Celtic Chieftainess, Mrs Donal O'Sullivan'. A suggestion that Sir Robert Tate, Junior Dean of Trinity College, had dressed up as Madame du Barry is probably intended to refer to Lady Tate. It seems that in those days it was safe to play with fire. A Madame de Pompadour dress made frequent appearances at such entertainments as these.

But there were signs abroad in Ireland of more significant stirrings than a penchant for fancy dress. In 1928, at the Peacock Theatre, Lower Abbey Street, the Dublin Gate Theatre studio gave its opening performance in public with Ibsen's *Peer Gynt*.

Mr Hilton Edwards, according to the report, gave us a very fine performance in the title role and Miss May Carey and Miss Coralie Carmichael were also praised for their performances. Lord Longford backed this new venture when the Gate Theatre opened at the Rotunda, and so long as he was prepared to meet the losses the company gave Dublin theatre of a high international standard. Orson Welles and James Mason made their first professional appearances at the Gate, but that was still in the future. At the Abbey, a young woman of Anglo-Irish parentage had founded a school of ballet. W. B. Yeats had ideas of linking all forms of dramatic art together; but Miss de Valois was a balletomane. She should have been kept in Dublin. In London she built up one of the greatest ballet companies in the world. But even now it would be impossible to finance an undertaking on that scale. We could hardly hope to have kept Miss de Valois by clipping her wings.

Dublin was as theatrically-minded then as now. There were several theatre groups, notably the Drama League and the New Players. Madame Kirkwood Hackett organized a scratch company, sometimes with bizarre results, as when at her cry for 'her little blue book' she was furnished by the stage manager with a copy of Thom's Directory. The private houses' – the Reddins and Mrs Kennedy Cahill's – theatricals were a regular form of entertainment. The healing efforts of the McNeills and the political support Mr Cosgrave received from the substantial remnant of former ascendancy neither accomplished nor evidenced any basic change in loyalties. Support for the new régime came from the head, not the heart. This was sufficiently demonstrated at the first military jumping competition for the Aga Khan trophy at the 1928 Horse Show, when the cheers that greeted the British team – which incidentally, contained two Irishmen, Brigadier Boylan and Colonel Hume-Dudgeon – were prodigious. And when the British anthem was played, a deafening chorus broke from the members stand where the occupants rose to their feet and sang to a man. With one exception: Lord Longford, who retained his seat and his hat, had the latter struck off by an enthusiastic loyalist. God Save the King was dangerous playing in those days when Armistice Day was a source of endless contention. The past was too near, for everybody. In 1930 the King's health was still being drunk in Trinity College. I was present at the supper after the inaugural meeting of the College Historical Society when Eoin O'Mahony substituted Ireland for the royal toast. Owen Sheehy Skeffington was one of Mr O'Mahony's most vigorous supporters in the ensuing rumpus, the echoes of which reverberated down the years. But that toast was never given again.

It had been the custom to play God Save the King at the Trinity College Sports until Mr McNeill, acting without the advice of the Executive Council, declined to be present if it was played. Thereupon it dropped from the College repertoire. With Mr de Valera's accession to office in 1932 many feared that a social as well as a political revolution was about to take place. One who expressed this fear to Arthur Clery, a clever, sweet-tempered, uncompromising republican, was reassured. 'It is only a change from government by Clongowes men to government by Christian Brothers men', he said. If the anxious questioner was a Trinity man he might have been astonished at one ultimate result of the change of government. The close connection between University College and Government was broken. In the long run Trinity College was to benefit from the change.

Apart from the political changes which Mr de Valera had pledged himself to bring about, there were also social consequences from his election. His government took office after a world economic crash as sudden as it was far-reaching. It heralded a new era with Fascism in Europe, the collapse of the parliamentary Labour party in Britain, and a more humane social policy in the United States. With its industrial policy, the new government preached a doctrine of republican austerity. The silk hat, as a symbol of reaction, was proscribed for ceremonious wear by Ministers. At the Eucharistic Congress in 1932, Mr de Valera and his cabinet colleagues were conspicuous in black soft hats and short coats. This departure from international convention gave the wits an opportunity of which they were not slow to avail themselves. More than to-day Dublin was the spiteful, unmannerly town of Yeats's description. As well as realities, people fought over symbols. The top-hat came to represent the crown which Mr de Valera was anxious to remove from the constitution.

This involved the Government in unhappy relations with Mr McNeill, the Governor-General, who refused to co-operate in the virtual suppression of his office. Relations between Merrion Street and the Park, long simmering, boiled over eventually. In the process a party at the French Legation was made the centre of a scene. On the appearance of Mr McNeill, who had been ordered to keep house, the various Ministers present hustled out their wives, all in new dresses – some of them left in tears. It was an abrupt ending to what promised to be a gay evening.

One of the immediate consequences of the subsequent abolition of Mr McNeill's office was the extinction of a place where visitors from abroad could meet our leaders, and our leaders could meet people whose interests were not exclusively political. But even without a stamping ground in the Park, a social background to the grim contemporary scene was provided by the legations. Here, for example, is the record of an historical occasion that might escape the attention of the pedagogue. The date is August 1932. The source the *Irish Tatler and Sketch*.

Mr Orr-Denby, the secretary to the United States Legation, and Mrs Denby, have taken a charming house in Ailesbury Road where, during the month, they gave their first cocktail party. It was a most enjoyable affair, and a new idea to Dublin – we have had so few of these American parties yet in the City. Cocktails with the accompaniment of chips and almonds, tiny onions, olives and sandwiches, as an appetiser to those going home to dinner, have recently been the vogue in London.

A sandwich is unlikely to whet the appetite for dinner, but the controversy in this innocent prattle, lay in the loaded phrase *to those going home to dinner*. For, at that time, there were two schools of eating: those who maintained the provincial tradition of high tea. It was essentially a silent struggle, hostilities never flared up in the open. But it led to embarrassments. Those who had brought to the city the ways of the country refused to change them, and to dine late, like wearing a top hat, was a symptom of political unsoundness.

Mrs Orr-Denby's innovation took time to catch on. It was not usual to serve drinks apart from meals, and at entertainments other than dinners and suppers, guests were satisfied to take afternoon tea. Women drank very little. The great salon of the period over which Miss Sarah Purser presided at Mespil House was conducted on principles of economy which would have won the approval of Lady Aberdeen.

Miss Purser issued a general invitation to anyone who met with her approval to come to these monthly entertainments. An iron character, Miss Purser overrode all prejudices of a trivial kind, and the qualifications she sought in her guests was their capacity to interest her. It is largely due to her – she enlisted Dr Bodkin in the enterprise – that we have the Municipal Gallery in Charlemont House. She founded the Friends of the National Collections and established the only course in Fine Arts that we have in the two Dublin Colleges. Lady Fingall who, in other days, used to act as hostess for that ill-treated patriot, Sir Horace Plunkett, at Kilteragh Lodge, kept a small salon after his death. Her entertainments were weekly. And there one met the survivors of the Kilteragh days, of whom Senator George O'Brien, Professor of Economics in University College, was one, Dr Richard Best, evoking memories of George Moore, another. Of active politicians I can only recall Desmond FitzGerald and, at a later date, Frank Mac-Dermot. Lady Fingall had not emancipated herself completely from the past and kept, I always thought, its fallen day about her. She complained about the dinner-table conversation of Cabinet Ministers and said she had become tired of prison experiences as a topic. Quite charming, she was not defenceless. Woe betide anyone brash enough to assume that a pass was issued when she said she was at home on *every* Thursday.

The tennis party on Saturday and Sunday afternoons (in Protestant homes, not Sunday, as a rule) was a very popular entertainment. The standard of play was rarely high, but a tennis court provided an economic way of entertaining all save the infirm.

Neither of the Universities played much part in general society. Dr Walter Starkie was an exception: his interests were diverse, his instincts gregarious and hospitable. He was rather frowned upon in Trinity which sympathized more with Sir Robert Tate's liking for undergraduate entertainments. Serious artists find society a waste of time except in so far as it provides copy. Dublin was very rich in talent at the beginning of this decade. Yeats at the Abbey, A.E. editing *The Irish Statesman,* Sean O'Casey, a sensational discovery, Gogarty enlivening society and envenoming politics, James Stephens sitting at the feet of A.E. By the end of the decade all had gone away. A.E.'s paper ruined by long drawn out litigation, Gogarty crushed by a libel action. The thirties was an era of libel proceedings by writers and against writers – a time of dying lions.

England was too much on the national mind. If some hankered after the old and were unable to throw off social subservience to England, others only had to know what was done in England to prescribe the opposite. It was necessary to forget England, and that would take time. Only in the Gate Theatre were we in touch with an outside world. Dermot O'Brien, President of the Royal Hibernian Academy, a generous encourager of youth, patron as well as painter, discharged his duties in the academic style and was an admirable host. But artistic taste in Dublin remained static. Jack Yeats found it hard to sell his later pictures and, if lip service was paid to W.B. Yeats, his later poems were not generally appreciated. Bourgeois Dublin has no time for artists and sneered at Yeats in private, while the paintings of his brother were regarded as a joking matter. Let us recall the fashionable journalist. This is taken at random from a guide to visitors to Dublin in 1932.

The Country Shop – St. Stephen's Green. A bright and jolly little haunt for tea and talk, where a delightful atmosphere helps the digestion of those delicious potato-cakes which are a speciality here. Silver Slipper, 41 Harcourt Street. The only 'cheerio' spot open in Dublin after 11 or 12 o'clock where you can dance and sup and breakfast and be entertained by a snappy cabaret show, lounge and orchestra. Remodelled dance floor and a hostess, who keeps things zipping along! A lively spot to adjourn to after the show is over (stiff shirt advised but not essential).

Miss Muriel Gahan must have squirmed then as we now squirm at the style of the social gossip. But the silly side of life was outside the deep sources of conflict which find expression in Denis Johnston's play *The Old Lady Says No*.

There was a fundamental clash which was to prove ultimately more significant than political bitterness which would die with time and the growth of self-confidence. It is well illustrated by the division of opinion between two members of Mr Cosgrave's cabinet, the impossibility of reconciling the ideals of Kevin O'Higgins with the dreams of J.J. Walsh.

The latter, as Minister for Posts and Telegraphs, prophesied that a powerful radio transmitter in Athlone would sell Ireland as a tourist resort to the world. He had inspected the hotels of the Continent and considered that the Irish hotels of 1927 came up to their standard. In any event, it was necessary to say so, and the world, listening to Irish radio programmes, would hear it and believe it. It was he who gave Kevin O'Higgins, shortly before his death, a list of business men's names. They, he said, would be prepared to finance the political campaign of 1927 if they were promised protection for the industries they wanted to establish. O'Higgins, without reading it, put the list in the fire, and Walsh left the Government. The action of one showed a fastidiousness that is hard to reconcile with the acquisitive impulses of the common man. It made insufficient allowance for the eagerness of enterprise and opportunism without which there cannot be material progress. That enterprise and opportunism, if not checked by a reasonable insistence on high standards, leads to profit-seeking as the ultimate satisfaction, the whole aim and purpose of life was not present to the mind of the other. That crisis came at the beginning of that decade: it has not yet been resolved. Soon afterwards O'Higgins and his uncompromising idealism were shot out of existence outside the church in Bootersown.

In 1937 there were more cheerful auguries. The Economic War had been settled and Mr de Valera and Mr Neville Chamberlain would soon reach an accord based on mutual esteem. The new Constitution gave the opportunity for an imaginative appointment to the new office of president.

Dr Douglas Hyde, if he had not existed, might have been invented for the occasion. Founder of the Gaelic

League, unpolitical, poet, sportsman, Protestant, scholar of Trinity College, Professor at University College, Irish-speaking Anglo-Irishman; he was the kindest and least controversial of men. His appointment marked the first stage of political maturity; but in growing up we may have lost, with its passions, some of the innocence of youth.

DE VALERA IN POWER

Professor T. Desmond Williams

Mr. de Valera was elected parliamentary president of the executive council on March 9th 1932. At the time of taking office he had already been in politics for over twenty years. He was to go on for roughly twenty-five years more. This discussion concerns mainly the five years between his first nomination as head of the Free State government and his election under a new constitution in 1937. And it deals with the personality and policy of De Valera in power rather than with general political history in that time. Those first years, short as they were, are sufficient to indicate the main outlines of de Valera as a political animal, as the leader of a party. An English historian claimed that in many respects he was the most remarkable figure in post-Versailles Europe. He was the only one who assumed power as an apparent revolutionary, in a potentially revolutionary situation, and, having gained most of his political objectives by constitutional means, was to become outside a lasting symbol of representative democracy. Some measure of his impact is provided by the steady interest he aroused outside Ireland in the period under examination, and indeed until his retirement from party politics. De Valera and his colleagues stood abroad for what was taken to be the Irish Cause. This was so despite the fact that he never overcame the opposition of half the electorate.

The first weeks of his regime gave every sign of immanent social and political revolution. He and his deputies entered the Dail on March 9th with revolvers in their pockets, such was their distrust in the democratic intentions of the Cosgrave government. They feared a coup d'etat and the setting up of martial law by some of Cosgrave's ministers, and, more particularly, by some leaders of the Free State army. In spite of all the rumours, these suspicions proved to be unfounded. Proceedings in the new Dail followed the constitutional pattern and de Valera, initially supported by Fianna Fail, Labour and James Dillon, now found himself in a position to implement the social and economic programmes he had been preaching for so long. What were they?

Firstly there was the rejection of the oath of allegiance to the British sovereign and the introduction of widespread constitutional innovation; secondly the retention by an Irish government of land annuities hitherto paid to Britain. And thirdly he wanted intensified support for Irish industry, symbolised primarily by the Control of Manufacturers' Act of 1934, to be introduced principally by Sean Lemass, as minister of industry and commerce. Lastly came some extension of social services, pensions, and above all the transformation of agricultural society from grazing (or rather ranching, as it was controversially called) to tillage and further small holdings. Irish Ireland, of course, included the restoration of Gaelic, though this was not at the time an issue between the parties. This did not go particularly further. And since then not any further either.

To carry this programme through a majority was required in the Dail, accompanied by continuing electoral support and the co-operation of the civil service. De Valera had to confront Cumann na nGaedheal, a main opposition party – over-confident of its own competence and reckless in its belief that the government would collapse within a few months on account of the ignorance and inexperience of the new ministry. There was also a small Labour Party, whose support had to be won to maintain a parliamentary majority. Outside parliament de Valera had to deal with the extremer republican forces, who had voted for him – not as their leader, but to force him towards full scale republicanism, with all its national and, in many cases, socialist trappings. The I.R.A. had once been his friends. It was only by way of de Valera that they thought the Free State government could be overthrown. They had fought beside him during the civil war ten years before, but they had never accepted the reality or possibility of constitutional processes. For them the army remained the sole source of government. And as from 1934 they were to

31

quote the de Valera of 1922 against the de Valera of 1932.

If the Dail worked formally within traditional procedure, things were very different in the countryside. Violence and murder between 1927 and 1932 had taken their passionate, if sporadic toll. Though temporarily suppressed by public safety acts under Cosgrave, sentiments of anger spread through the countyside. Leaders of the post-1932 opposition were shouted down, and sometimes beaten up in such counties as Cork, Limerick, Kerry and Mayo. Action and reaction being equal und opposite, the Army Comrades' Association, composed mainly of former free state officers, was then founded to secure a free platform for the new opposition. Each side blamed the other for the illegalities and physical incidents that threatened to shallow the country.

In the Dail then de Valera had to deal with Cumann na nGaedheal, labour, and the farmers' party (subsequently established by James Dillon and Frank McDermott). Outside were the I.R.A. and the Army Comrades' Association, (or blue shirts to come). In addition he had to introduce his new social and economic programme. To all these problems were added the consequences of the so-called economic war, initiated by non-payment of the land annuities to Britain and 'Jimmy' Thomas's reaction. What had hitherto been a domestic struggle now became entangled with the older Anglo-Irish feud. The government at Westminster retaliated by imposing substantial tariffs on Irish goods entering the British market and soon offered commonwealth arbitration; de Valera was willing to accept the Hague Court of Justice. This wrangle went on for five years. The dispute was largely unnecessary; for the former railwayman Thomas was more Tory than many Tories. It cost the Irish economy many millions, though it is hard to assess the figure exactly. The loss certainly contributed to the destruction of one section of the community – that is the graziers. It facilitated the adoption of tillage, and it also placed de Valera firmly at the head of yet another conflict with the British. There is no reason to suppose that he had planned or foreseen this particular course. But in the outcome he was to extract one of his greatest victories from this conflict. In March 1938, as part of the final solution of this matter, the Irish government agreed to pay ten million pounds, in settlement of outstanding claims between the two countries. On the last day of these negotiations de Valera suddenly raised the question of the return of Irish naval bases occupied by British forces under a provision of the 1922 treaty. He had earlier concentrated on the old sore of Partition. Contrary to the expectations of all his diplomatic and professional advisers, Neville Chamberlain, the British prime minister, agreed to this bold proposal. From here grew the possibility of effective Irish neutrality in World War II. And out of apparent economic disadvantage a major diplomatic triumph was secured.

One of de Valera's notable political skills had been his capacity to conceal the precise nature of subsequent policy. He has rarely allowed either his colleagues or his opponents access to his inner political thoughts. The ambiguity of his statements on the republic and on foreign policy often exasperated his critics. They would have loved to pin him down on policies adopted in other and earlier circumstances. It looked as if he was always wanting the best of all worlds, however inconsistent these worlds might seemingly be. For de Valera politics was even then as it has been since an art with some scientific method in which nothing is ever black or white, all ways and means a shifting grey. Few politicians have paid more attention to the significance of detail in the use of words. All phrases were to be considered in the light of the use they might serve under altering circumstances. Hence the constant recurrence in those years of firm statements followed by intricate qualifications. His opponents indignantly regarded this practice as just another illustration of a devious Machiavellianism. Yet Machiavelli, fortunately or not, may be imitated with sincerity. De Valera rarely put himself forward as an anti-British crusader, but he certainly seemed one to many of his followers; and he entertained constant distrust of British policy when guided subsequently by Churchill. Yet some members of the British government, and of the civil service, regarded him as fundamentally on the side of the values for which Britain, along with other western democracies, thought that they stood for in any forthcoming world conflict.

To return to the home front – in 1933 de Valera was to turn first against extra-parliamentary sections of the opposition. The blue shirts are the subject of a separate chapter. The concern here is with the general handling of that crisis. Cosgrave and his colleagues opposed the abandoning of the oath, the curtailing, and eventual elimination of the role of governor general, and, at first, the abolition of payment to Britain of the land annuities. On all these matters they were forced into the position of appearing to support ministerial and parliamentarian attitudes as expressed in London. And the Cosgrave party still and initially commanded a majority in the senate.

De Valera went again to the country in 1933 and was returned to office this time with a small but adequate majority. No European democratic party since 1914, however well or ill-grounded its case, can afford to take refuge behind the supporting judgement of an upper chamber – be it senate, upper chamber, or house of lords – once the electorate has, for a second time, returned a government advocating policies unacceptable to that upper house. It simply won't work. It is at this point that the political wisdom of the new opposition in both houses could be queried. There are some parties, or it may be leaders, that are better equipped for government than for opposition; others can face both situations. Cumann na nGaedheal, though it led well, did not oppose well; it seemed to think that its past record was enough. But electorates are only interested in the future.

At this time too cracks were appearing in the hitherto homogenous façade of the opposition. The commissioner of police, General O'Duffy, formerly a close friend of Michael Collins and Kevin O'Higgins, was dismissed from the force in February 1933. The Cosgraveites looked like losing their nerves. De Valera had come back again. How could they ever get him out? O'Duffy joined the pre-existing Army Comrades' Association almost immediately. This group had been founded in 1931-32 for the purpose of maintaining free speech on the streets against I.R.A. extremists. He was accepted as their leader on July 20th. As the new director general, he announced that the national guard (new name for the A.C.A.) would have an official uniform: the blue shirt. He also stated that the national guard would have physical drill... 'to be practised only as a means of promoting good health, character and discipline.'

A month later O'Duffy proclaimed the holding of a guard parade in Merrion Square, marching past Leinster lawn. The parade was banned by government order, the national guard declared to be an unlawful organisation, and a military tribunal set up – a tribunal of the kind so strongly denounced by de Valera when in opposition. De Valera may have panicked but the precedent of the march on Rome was there, and O'Duffy and Commandant Cronin did laud Fascist exemplars. On September 8th the Cosgrave party and the farmers', or national centre party joined forces with O'Duffy. The result was called the United Ireland party. O'Duffy, who held no seat in parliament, was to be its leader, and the vice-presidents were Cosgrave, James Dillon and Frank McDermott. The banned national guard was then renovated on allegedly constitutional lines. Its new title became The Young Ireland Association – as a legitimate branch of United Ireland. In November the new party issued a statement of policy, including the establishment of a corporate state (to some extent anyhow) and, curiously enough, the abolition of the existing proportional representative system of voting. Strong government required single seat constituencies.

Blue shirts were now the fashion, though the Young Ireland Association was by no means restricted to the young. Many middle aged and respectable leaders of the defunct Cumann na nGaedheal party sported the new uniform. Professors were attached to O'Duffy's personal staff and collaborated in writing his speeches, though he rarely kept to his script. John A. Costello was reported as saying that 'we have had the brownshirts, the black shirts and the greenshirts. In Ireland we are now going to have the blue shirts'. But there was no real unity of aim in this conglomerate United Ireland party. Cumann na nGaedheal, under Cosgrave, had stood for an established past; no one really knew what the future policies of the new party would be. O'Duffy was talking of fascism, as well as the corporate state. W.B. Yeats, for example, along with his friend Captain MacManus, was gloating in the Kildare Street Club over the prospects of a really virile fascist Irish state. Cosgrave was too nice to quarrel publicly with all this and McDermott distrusted the new director general, and was distrusted by him.

The history of the blue shirts does not last very long. It ended virtually in the late summer of 1934. O'Duffy's proposal that farmers should not pay the land annuities to their own government, and that others should not pay their rates, led to a crisis within the United Ireland party. The first to raise revolt against the General – or, as he put it, against his generally destructive and hysterical leadership – was James Hogan, professor of history in University College, Cork. O'Duffy was way in advance of his party; if he managed to keep some of his troops, he lost the staff at headquarters. 'Give them the lead' O'Duffy had been a successful if loquacious O.C. in the northern I.R.A. As a Commissioner of Police he had shown creative administrative power, as a polical leader he was a rumbustious child. For him there then afterwards remained the tragic comedy of the Irish Brigade in Spain.

The blue shirt movement enabled de Valera to accuse his opponents of flirtation with fascism, and of opposition to democracy. Instead of ejecting him, it strengthened his position enormously. It also enabled him to maintain an increasingly uneasy connection with the I.R.A. Most important of all it gave him the opportunity (whether he sought it or not) of using a military tribunal – first against his political foes, and then, when it became necessary, against the I.R.A. It would have been much more difficult for him to have applied the so-called coercion act of 1931 against the I.R.A., if he had not first secured their support in using it against the blue shirts. O'Duffy was soon dealt with. De Valera waited far longer – indeed until 1936, before moving against the I.R.A.

The I.R.A. merits separate treatment, not as a power-ful political movement but as a symbol of forces, emotions and ideals associated with the whole history of Ireland since the Fenians. They represented full-blooded republicanism, which, put in its most simple form, might be reduced to:

1. The securing of a republican form of government,
2. The establishment of a united thirty-two county Ireland,
3. The elimination of British armed forces from both the north and the south,
4. The achievement of all these aims by force rather than by the more patient processes of persuasion.

The I.R.A. also refused to make use of their country's parliament. Most of their leaders shared a disposition towards socialism, as they understood it, or towards what was then regarded as communism. The Bolsheviks were among the first to recognise the government set up by the first Dail in 1919: in 1925 Sean Lemass had sent emissaries – as republican minister of defence – to meet Soviet agents in Berlin. This had nothing to do with socialist or communist ideologies. It was simply a question of discovering provisional interests against a common foe. But the republicans of the thirties – Michael Price and Peadar O'Donnell – wished to link a war against property with the war against the British and their Irish 'tools'.

United as the I.R.A. were on the nationalist programme, they could never agree on social and economic policies. Many had lived on the excitement of being on the run with a gun. Some also, on account of their youthful experiences, found it difficult to come to terms with bourgeois society. In this they were not so unlike the groups that crowded around revolutionary figures in Munich and Milan after the first world war. They were idealists, without sense of law or order. To some extent they lived in a dreamland which only became reality under some impact of violence applied from within or without. All were courageous, as they pictured courage. They were gay and generous with their own and grim to the stranger who was not attuned to their political philosophy. Hence the perpetual recurrence of conspiracy whenever a friend stepped out of line, the threatened treachery and the personal rancours. Hence too the constant appearance of breakaway splinter groups. In some respects they were like the revolutionary emigrants from Poland or Russia in the western Europe of the late nineteenth and early twentieth centuries. Some never got over the fear of police spies or agents provocateurs. Some, as they grew older, began to doubt not the purity of their ideals, but the efficacy of the means employed. It was de Valera's success in maintaining and extending his authority in a constitutional manner that undermined confidence in their case. Anyhow between 1932 and 1936 Peadar O'Donnell, Frank Ryan, Maurice Twomey, the Gilmore brothers, Michael Price and lesser leading lights were starting to bicker over ways and means of attaining their stated goals. Some saw de Valera as the great betrayer, the man who had led them and left them; others felt he had outwitted them for good. There were the occasional Nechaevs – men who, following the pattern of the Russian social revolutionary movement, believed in terror as an instrument of policy, and in their unsophisticated subtlety, thought that terror, by provoking counterterror would gain them sympathy. Sean McBride and Maurice Twomey, probably the ablest of the leaders (though in very different ways) gradually moved towards constitutional methods. Twomey from within jail, McBride still outside it. The I.R.A. had been very busy, but to what account? Two murders appalled the country: Richard More O'Farrell, Edgeworthstown, committed on February 9th, 1935: Vice-Admiral Somervill, Castletowns-end, March 24th, 1936. From March 1935 the I.R.A. started shooting in earnest against de Valera's civic guards. The army council of the I.R.A. attempted to join forces with transport strikers. The long predicted and long postponed conflict was now on. Still De Valera moved slowly, reprieving and commuting death sentences on I.R.A. men.

The I.R.A. was not disposed of in 1936. It was to resurrect itself dangerously throughout World War II. The danger then lay in the field of international relations. But it had ceased to be a major issue in domestic politics by 1938. Government and opposition were now agreed on this. The fact remains that de Valera never showed himself indignant about the motives of these men to the national left. Some, arrested in 1936, later released, resuming violence during the war, were subsequently executed. Certain deeds and deaths here seemed to touch him deeply.

The subject of de Valera in power involves some judgement on his conduct of less bitter affairs. When he first took office, he and his team were certainly inexperienced. The civil service did what they could to train the new government. Many of his followers including ministerial colleagues, distrusted the civil service, led as it was sometimes by departmental secretaries, working under a free state government, and a previous British administration. Between the result of the election in February 1932 and de Valera's nomination as president of the executive council in March, the civil service was instructed to do nothing that would give the new government any grounds for believing their service to be connected with any political party. In certain departments prominent secretaries went so far as to abandon the close personal relationships they had personally held with members of the Cosgrave cabinet. This should only have occurred in what was feared to be a near-revolutionary situation. Under the circumstances it was probably desirable, and certainly successful. The new government was as faithfully attended by its servants as its predecessors had been. The names of McElligott, Walsh, Murphy, Moynihan, Andrews, and Leyden mattered then, or subsequently.

De Valera in power was concerned with his cabinet, his party, his parliament – and, from time to time, with the foreign scene. As a party leader, his success was beyond dispute. He controlled his cabinet tightly, yet he made room for differing shades of opinion. He rarely allowed votes; and waited upon the arrival of a 'consensus' of opinion arrived at by his own superb sense of tactics. No one dared oppose him, but he did not object to ministerial differences. Not that any of his ministers wished to disagree much. Lemass from the very beginning withstood the parliamentary assaults of the opposition and ran his ministry, sometimes rudely and roughly, but with effect. In the Dail he always gave at least as good as he got. Sean I. O'Kelly, though despised by his political opponents, knew a great deal about housing and popular sentiment. The opposition judged him by a more exuberant statement in 1938 about how 'he whipped John Bull every time. Look at our last agreement. We won all round us; we wiped her right, left and centre, and with God's help we shall do the same again.' This was preposterously far-fetched. It was not met with opposing humour. McEntee was competent on whatever job he was in. He was commonly regarded as the hatchet man of the party. If so, he was most successful in winning elections. Aiken, as minister of finance, was much more highly thought of by the dour and suspicious men in the department of finance than his agile counter parts on the front bench opposition seemed to think. He was the only one to make generous remarks about the men on the other side in the civil war.

De Valera had his left wing and his right wing, his radical and his conservative colleagues. He looked principally to the preservation of a society represented by the small farmer. He never quite understood nor favoured an industrial revolution, but in a political situation in which all issues ultimately ended with DEV OR NO DEV he found no real difficulty in allowing contrary trends to take their course. In parliament he sometimes lost his temper in the earlier years and on occasion engaged in vituperative comments on political opponents. He allowed himself to accuse Mulcahy of treasonable talks with the British secretary of state for war. Later he withdrew the charge without dignity and without generosity. Sometimes in those early years he was to display a public sensitivity that was rarely allowed to appear after World War II. At times a personal battle took place between the gifted Professor McGilligan and his colleague in the National University, Chancellor de Valera. But on the whole the President of the executive council allowed others to engage in this type of disagreement. Between 1932 and 1938 de Valera set himself three main tasks: the abolition of the oath, the abolition of the governor general, and the introduction of a new constitution. That constitution was

40

intended to represent, regarding 'external association' and internal organisation of society the aims he had proclaimed in earlier years. In prosecuting these tasks and in maintaining the constitutional authority of his own party he showed three obvious qualities: patience, persistence and an acute sense of timing. He also knew how to take advantage of his opponents' mistakes, and despite the shifts and ambiguities of policy kept the loyalty of most who had really supported him in 1932.

But he was also to win new friends. He had become during and after the civil war a political revolutionary. In social and economic affairs he proved as leader of the government a conservative. There were no shattering innovations regarding property, finance or religion. The banking commission of 1934-38 illustrated some of this, and here again the civil service was involved. The composition of its members, and its final report, published after a well-timed election in June 1938, demonstrated most clearly that de Valera stood for social evolution on the basis of the status quo, once over the constitutional hurdles. Meanwhile by 1938 the ending of partition and the restoration of the Irish language were as far from fulfilment as ever.

THE BLUESHIRTS

David Thornley

In the spring of 1931 an organization of ex-members of the Free State Army, the Army Comrades Association, was formed under the leadership of Dr. T.F. O'Higgins. In August 1932 the Association opened its ranks to the public; in a few weeks it claimed a membership of 30,000, and eighteen months later, 100,000. In April 1933, shortly after the second general election in twelve months had confirmed Mr de Valera's position as President of the Executive Council, the association adopted as a distinctive mark of its membership the wearing of a blue shirt. In July 1933 the A.C.A. took a new name, that of the National Guard, and a new leader, General Eoin O'Duffy, who had been dismissed from the Commissionership of the Civic Guard the previous February. In September 1933 the National Guard joined with Cumann na nGaedheal and the National Centre Party in a new political movement, United Ireland, or, in its Irish and soon more popularly used equivalent, Fine Gael, under the presidency of General O'Duffy. Almost exactly a year later General O'Duffy resigned. By 1935 Fine Gael had much the same leadership, and much the same political identity, as had Cumann na nGaedheal.

The so-called Blueshirt movement occupied a central place in Irish politics for less than two years. Yet few Irish political movements have left such a legacy of controversy. To their opponents the Blueshirts were fascists from whom only stern action by the government and the hostility of the I.R.A. saved Irish democracy. To the surviving supporters of the movement it was an association forced into existence by the circumstance that after the 1932 election the men who had governed Ireland for a decade were denied freedom of speech by the mob violence of I.R.A. and Fianna Fáil supporters.

Which, if either, is the explanation of Blueshirtism? To attempt to answer that question one must delve back into a time of unfulfilled hopes, of bitterness, and of political instability.

The 1932 election was remarkable in that it returned to political power a leader who less than ten years before had been in arms against the parliamentary state. Mr Cosgrave's cabinet gave way to men whom it could regard in all sincerity as erstwhile revolutionaries and assassins. The new cabinet stared across at men, many of whom it regarded as bloody executioners. Government ministers could describe the men from whom they took the seals of office as traitors in the tradition of Castlereagh and Carey; the weekly newspaper of the opposition found no distaste in caricaturing the leader of the new government as a Spanish gunman. The complete distrust of government and opposition for each other's intentions is the most fundamental explanation of the events of 1933 and 1934.

This distrust was heightened by the fact that Mr de Valera was returned to power with the almost unanimous enthusiasm of the I.R.A. It was an enthusiasm doomed inevitably to wither, for the I.R.A. made it quite clear that even if Mr de Valera were to 'chop off some of the imperial tentacles like the oath and the Governor-Generalship, it would never 'give allegiance to a cabinet which accepts or functions within the British Empire'. But the links which bound the Republican army to Fianna Fáil were emotionally strong for all that. The rank and file of the two organizations possessed shared recollections, social backgrounds, and often family ties. They could see no analogy between the Republican Army and the developing Blueshirt movement. 'The I.R.A. has its roots since the Anglo-Normans came to Ireland', said one Fianna Fáil Deputy as late at March 1934: 'The I.R.A. represent the people.'

This tacit alliance was not confined to the prosecution of short-term constitutional objectives. In the small farming communities, Fianna Fáil members had joined in the agitation against payment of the land annuities with members of Saor Eire, the political organization which had sprouted from the I.R.A. in 1931. Saor Eire's advocacy of socialism, republicanism, and land division made it an organization soon condemned as communist by the Catholic hierarchy and as subversive by the government. But above all else, Fianna Fáil and the I.R.A. were at one in their desire to free the Republicans imprisoned by the Cosgrave administration. 'Open the gaol gates' was the great cry of this election. For the moment it transcended the niceties of constitutional disagreement.

But it soon became clear that the I.R.A. saw Mr de Valera's triumph as a stage in a republican struggle against British imperialism and that a large element in it was thoroughly imbued with socialist principle. To the socialist republican the fight against imperialism was inseparable from the fight against capitalism. Connolly and Mellowes were the two great apostles of this tradition. The oath, and indeed the border, were not the only pieces of unfinished business.

The result was that the Fianna Fáil cabinet was embarrassed by the enthusiasm of the republican left on three issues. The decision of the new government to withold the land annuities from Britain but to continue to collect them in whole or in part did not go nearly far enough to satisfy the agrarian socialists of the I.R.A. Secondly, the promotion of native private enterprise by tariff protection did little to meet the appeals of *An Phoblacht,* the I.R.A. newspaper, for 'the squelching of the old gang'. 'War on the ranches and the banks', demanded *An Phoblacht:* 'The banks to be taken over and made to serve the interests of the people, not of their overlords. The ranches to be divided and distributed. Only when these things are done will the economic stranglehold of imperialism be loosened.' For a brief few years the tempo of European slump politics seemed to be reproduced in Ireland as the interests of big and small farmer, capitalist and socialist and corporativist, clashed to the cry of 'Rancher', 'Fascist', 'Communist'. Professor James Hogan, one of the principal theoreticians of the United Ireland Party, produced a series of articles on communism in Ireland in the party newspaper in 1933 and 1934 which were subsequently developed in a celebrated pamphlet, *Could Ireland become Communist?* In this series Saor

Éire, the I.R.A., the left wing Republican Congress of 1934, and even those in the I.R.A. who opposed the Republican Congress, were identified as communist or 'communistic', while Fianna Fáil itself was repeatedly accused of a Kerensky-like softness on communism. These fears were grossly exaggerated, but they were widely and often sincerely held. They contributed to the sense of physical peril which the supporters of the Cosgrave government already felt in the face of the untested constitutionalism of Fianna Fáil. 'One thing, at all events, is certain', wrote Professor Hogan in November 1933: 'It was the growing menace of the Communist I.R.A. that called forth the Blueshirts as inevitably as Communist anarchy called forth the Blackshirts in Italy.'

But the most immediate issue which generated political tension in the summer of 1932 was perhaps the most simple. Every physical force conflict leaves its memories of atrocity, and it was widely expected, both by the I.R.A. and in Fianna Fáil, that heads would now roll in the police. When the flood of expected dismissals was not immediately forthcoming, the rank and file were puzzled and resentful. Fianna Fáil cumainn passed resolutions of protest, one cumann, with a certain disingenuousness, declared that if the government would not dismiss a particularly disliked judge, it might at least remove his police guard. In retrospect it can be seen that Mr de Valera acted with great restraint, and the Minister for Justice, Mr Geoghegan, a distinguished K.C. with a short record of political involvement, earned much unpopularity with his own supporters as a result. But the removal first of Colonel David Neligan and then, in February 1933, of General O'Duffy himself, added to the fears of the opposition. If they were to be brought into collision with the Republican left, how far could they depend for physical protection upon a police force which was already undermanned and now, in their opinion, the object of political pressures.

Such a collision scarcely seemed a remote possibility in 1932 and 1933. Freedom of speech was an exotic concept in post-civil war Ireland. Mr Cosgrave was howled down in Cork in May 1932 and a meeting which he attempted to address in Dublin the following January was forcibly broken up. A County Wicklow cumann of Fianna Fáil called for the restriction of statements and publications 'calculated to lessen the Irish people's confidence in the Irish government and in each other, or to discourage, dishearten and weaken the Irish people in any way or give information to the enemy.' The breaking-up of Cumann na nGaedheal meetings was the reason given for the formation of the Army Comrades Association and its adoption of a distinctive uniform. In turn, when ex-Commissioner O'Duffy assumed its leadership, he at once declared that his new followers 'did not support the view that Communists should be free to organize'. The word Communist was pretty comprehensive in the Ireland of the 1930's.

As the year 1933 drew on the physical struggle escalated. One section of the press carried reports of I.R.A. outrages, the other, pictures of captured Blueshirt batons and knuckle-dusters. In the middle sat the successive Ministers for Justice, Mr Geoghegan and Mr Ruttledge, accused with equal force by both sides of partiality towards the other. By mid-1933 there were two private armies in Ireland. One was convinced of its historic continuity from Pearse and from the Republican Dáil. It was un-uniformed, but well-armed, and enjoyed, as yet, strong ties of affinity with the supporters of the government. The other was convinced that it was defending order and religion against a weak and partial government and a socialist I.R.A. This army was less well-quipped with firearms, but it displayed a uniform, a salute, and a set of slogans evocative of the violent politics of the European continent. It was equipped, after July 1933, with a leader who was energetic, eloquent, and totally without experience of political responsibility.

O'Duffy at first refused to allow the National Guard to be openly associated with any party; 'party politics', he was reported as saying, 'has served its period of usefulness.' It is not, then, perhaps surprising that the tensest moment in the short history of the movement occurred *before* it became affiliated with Fine Gael. O'Duffy proposed to commemorate the deaths of Kevin O'Higgins and Michael Collins with a mass march to Glasnevin on 13 August 1933.

Special trains were to carry country contingents to Dublin; at least three to four thousand uniformed Blueshirts were expected to march. The analogy with Mussolini was not lost, and rumours of an impending *coup d'état* circulated despite the strenuous denials of O'Duffy. The government retaliated by confiscating the arms held under licence by the leading members of the movement throughout the country, and by the ex-ministers of the Cosgrave government. It also speeded up the recruitment of a special police force composed principally of ex-I.R.A. men of congenial political sympathies. Cumann na nGaedheal protested bitterly in the Dáil against the arms seizures, contrasting them sharply with the tacit acceptance of the I.R.A.'s retention of its armament; it questioned also the fitness of the new police force for its responsibilities. Recruitment was, however, pressed on. By 4 August 1933 some of the 'Broy Harriers', as they were nicknamed after the new police chief, were already patrolling in the vicinity of Leinster House. On the night of Saturday 12 August the government met to take a final decision on the march. At 12.50 a.m. on Sunday it was banned. The government was uncertain that O'Duffy would have the time, or the will, to cancel it. Three hundred Gardaí ringed Leinster House; seven hundred lined the route of the march; about one hundred were at Glasnevin; further units patrolled the railway platforms. But early on Sunday morning O'Duffy called off his men, protesting both at the decision and its short notice. Apart from a few baton charges in O'Connell Street, Sunday 13 August passed off quietly.

O'Duffy was adamant that no coup had been intended; Mr Cosgrave called the suggestion 'fantastic nonsense'. But the acceptance of the ban caused a loss of face akin to O'Connell's abandonment of the Clontarf meeting in 1843. This may have been a contributory factor in persuading the previously sceptical O'Duffy to accept an open alliance with Cumann na nGaedheal and the Centre Party.

Efforts to bring the two principal opposition parties in the Dáil together before the 1933 election had proved unsuccessful, and as late as August 1933, Mr Frank MacDermott, leader of the Centre Party, had spoken critically of the embryonic corporativism which the General was beginning to enunciate. But two successive election defeats cast serious doubts upon the capacity of the opposition to shift Fianna Fáil; the Centre Party was clearly dividing the farming vote in the East and Midlands, and mounting violence enhanced the opposition's feeling of exposure. Some of the leaders of the Centre Party were also apparently still reluctant to submerge their identity beneath the twice-vanquished banner of Mr Cosgrave. But the personality of O'Duffy was available – attractive, eloquent, a martyr of government interference, and by repute an organizing genius. O'Duffy was elected president of the new alliance. It was a choice which all concerned were to regret within a twelvemonth.

The blueshirted National Guard was retained, also under O'Duffy's leadership, as the new party's youth movement. Every member of it was automatically a member of Fine Gael, but members of Fine Gael were by no means necessarily members of the youth movement. Some of the older Fine Gael members periodically wore blue shirts; many did not. The youth movement organized local sections, marched in uniform to its own meetings and those of its elders, and at them engaged in mutual fisticuffs with its opponents in which, at least by the end of 1933, it would be hard to say who provoked, or won, more often. There were girls' sections, which ran dances, and boys' sections, in which proud six-year-olds displayed themselves in uniform. Above this activity, the political courses of Fine Gael continued, under Mr Cosgrave's parliamentary leadership, much as before. There was, however, one theoretical difference. With the marching and counter-marching there went, in some quarters, a new emphasis on the superiority of the corporative system to that of party government. 'The blue shirt spells the end of laissez-faire and all the shibboleths of liberalism', wrote one contributor in *United Ireland,* the Fine Gael party newspaper, in October 1933. 'The intelligent young men of today... want discipline and efficiency, not individualism run mad', wrote another. The new Fine

Gael policy issued in November 1933 called for the establishment of economic corporations with statutory powers alongside the machinery of the state. They would by no means supplant parliamentary democracy, but 'strikes and lock-outs would become a thing of the past'.

Corporativist theories received their most sophisticated exposition in the writings in *United Ireland* of Professor Hogan and Professor Michael Tierney. 'Only in one country, Italy, is there any sign of an attempt to create out of the wreckage both of Parliament and party a really well-defined and complex machinery for dealing with a complex situation', wrote Professor Tierney in *United Ireland,* 16 December 1933. 'It is a complete mistake to suppose that Italian Fascism is merely a crude individual or party dictatorship. It is a product of peculiar Italian conditions, unknown elsewhere, but it has gradually evolved a scheme of social and political organization which is quite certain as time goes on to be adapted to the needs of every civilized country. In that scheme, dictatorship has more and more given way to a new and more intelligent, because more subtly organized, democracy. Mussolini, when his time comes to retire, will be succeeded, not by another dictator, but by a new entity suited to the needs of modern civilization, the Corporate State...

The Corporate State must come in the end in Ireland, as elsewhere.'

But the corporate state of the *United Ireland* intellectuals was no mere reproduction of Mussolini's Italy. It was the vocational teaching of Pope Pius XI in the encyclical *Quadragesimo Anno* which they sought to put into practice, and to do that, as Professor Tierney wrote on 24 March 1934, it was 'not in the least necessary to share Mussolini's rather drastic and in some ways excessive views on the exclusive rights of the state.' This school of thought was in the mainstream of the Catholic teaching on subsidiarity and vocationalism which has left its mark upon the theoretical construction of the modern Irish Senate.

It was understandable, though, that in the heated atmosphere of the 1930's, the distinction was sometimes lost on the members of Fianna Fáil, the I.R.A., and in particular the Labour party. Their confusion was made easier by the fact that some of the rank and file of the Blueshirt movement, and even at times the General himself, used much more violent language. O'Duffy could make half-a-dozen speeches asserting his devotion to democracy and to parliament, and then come out with the pronouncement that 'the State should fix the constitutions of the various unions and federations and take care that they are controlled by men of good character, public spirit, and sound national views.' At the lower strata of the movement a Hitlerian note was also sometimes to be heard. A correspondent named 'Oganach', writing in *United Ireland* in December 1933, suggested that Blueshirt audiences, instead of greeting their leader with a 'confused din', should imitate the Nazis, who 'give three sudden staccato bursts of mass cheering, each burst consisting of one sharply-ejected syllable... The word may be 'Heil!' (Hail!) pronounced sharply; or it may be Hoch! (Up!)... I can think of no single English word of one syllable to suggest for the purpose in mind', continued 'Oganach'. ' 'Hail!' would serve for receiving the Director-General and other dignitaries, but would not suit as an interjection indicating approval during the course of a speech or address. There may be Irish words of one syllable, capable of filling the mouth and being shot out powerfully. The matter is worthy of consideration. In addition to its touch of discipline (mental), it gives you another symbol by which you will differ from the herd.' I have no evidence that 'Oganach's' suggestion was seriously considered, although the ensuing issue of *United Ireland* bore a frontpage picture of O'Duffy on his release from a sojourn in Arbour Hill, with the caption 'Hail! O'Duffy!'.

It is doubtful, however, if this kind of display was taken very seriously by the leaders of the political movement. The corporativist theories passed over the heads of most people; the Mussolini-style posturings provided no more than an outlet for the physical energies of the sons of politically-minded elders. If it was a violent outlet, it was a violent age. It was also an age in which it was still possible to see Mussolini as the friend of the church, the founder of practical corporativism, the man who made the trains run on time. He was a man who had many respectable friends throughout Europe, who was not yet the open ally of Hitler's year-old regime in Germany. Parliamentary democracy was certainly in no danger from Mr. Cosgrave, who went on patiently speaking of constitutional and economic issues, half the time as if neither corporativism nor Blueshirts had ever existed. There is little evidence that more than one or two of the parliamentary leaders even took the corporativist theory very seriously. They were political leaders who had lost two elections in succession and did not want to lose a third; they had a simple and legitimate ambition: to oust Fianna Fáil. They chanced a bet on the charismatic personality of the General, and they lost.

If anyone took the uniforms and the salutes seriously, it was O'Duffy. He loved the demonstrations, loved the physical strain which constant hard work imposed on his boundless energies, loved oratory, and tended to be carried away by his own. A colleague once said to him: 'When you stick to your notes, General, you're the greatest speaker there is. But let some old woman in the audience shout 'Up Dev!', and God knows what you'll say next.' In the long run it was this euphoria which destroyed O'Duffy. He fell not because he was a fascist, which he may have been, insofar as the word is precisely meaningful, but because he was politically unstable.

He did not fall because the government overthrew him. The efforts of the Department of Justice to proscribe Blueshirtism were signally unsuccessful. The youth movement changed its name with O'Connellite dexterity and worsted the government in the courts. The government then introduced a bill to prohibit the wearing of uniforms. It was passed by the Dáil in March 1934 after a long debate which was marked by the violence of the exchanges, and by some unintentional moments of humour, as when Mr Fitzgerald Kenny described the bill, which empowered the police to remove the offending garment, as sending forth the Gardaí to tear the clothing off respectable Irish girls. The bill was rejected in the Senate; by the time when

51

it might have been reintroduced, O'Duffy's actions had made it superfluous.

By the spring of 1934 the tempo of the movement was, in fact, already slowing down. It had been able to capitalise on only one major social issue – the plight of the farmers, and especially the farmers of the Midlands, South, and East, in the economic war. Their resources depleted by declining markets and fresh tariff burdens, many formerly wealthy farmers withheld land annuities and rates. Large numbers of cattle were impounded for non-payment, and auctioned at a fraction of their value to mysterious buyers who arrived and disappeared chaperoned by armed Broy harriers. There were violent incidents, in one of which an unarmed youth was shot dead.

But the issue had two great disadvantages. In the first place, it did not attract *new* supporters to Fine Gael in sufficient number to topple the Fianna Fáil majority. In June 1934 the local elections brought the first test of the movement's electoral popularity. O'Duffy bombastically predicted, against the advice of his political lieutenants, that Fine Gael would sweep every county council in the Free State. In fact it won only eight out of twenty-three.

The second defect of the cattle-sales issue was its very violence. As the no-rates campaign mounted and the auctions continued, the farmers involved began to block roads and railways to impede them. In this course they had the sympathy and sometimes the aid of local blueshirts. The parliamentary leaders of Fine Gael would not condone illegal action against the state. But in August 1934 the first annual blueshirt congress in the Mansion House passed, with O'Duffy's approval, a resolution calling on the farmers to refuse to pay their annuities and on labourers not to pay their cottage rents. If that was not enough finally to provoke a constitutional political leadership already heartily sick of its bargain, the General emerged in County Cavan to announce that England was fortifying her outposts in the six counties and the Free State; if this meant war, said O'Duffy, he would be in it, and so would ninety-five per cent of the Blueshirts: 'The other five per cent should give up their shirts.'

These were the last two straws. On 31 August Professor Hogan resigned from the party, as a protest against 'the general destructive and hysterical leadership of its president'... On 21 September General O'Duffy was induced by the Central Council to resign from Fine Gael. O'Duffy subsequently denied that he had resigned from the Director-Generalship of the youth movement and set up a rival League of Youth, and subsequently, a National Corporative Party. Neither enjoyed any success. At the Ardfheis of Fine Gael in March 1935, Mr Cosgrave was elected to the vacant presidency; only one vocationalist resolution, declaring support for the principles of *Quadragesimo Anno,* was passed; it came from the League of Youth. In August the Congress of the League of Youth decided to democratise its constitution 'to alter the dictatorial status which had been given to the office of Director-General by a former holder.' In September the new constitution was published. In the list of the League's objects all reference to vocational or corporative organization had gone. Business was back to normal.

Was this brief episode a flirtation with fascism? Perhaps, as far as a small minority of the leaders and some of the rank and file were concerned. But throughout it all, the bulk of the leadership of Fine Gael remained solidly dedicated to parliamentary democracy. As one of O'Duffy's supporters wrote, the split showed the hunger of party politicians for 'the little traditional 'games' so dear to the profession.' He could not have paid them a finer compliment.

To the historian those eighteen months do sound some fascinating echoes of European politics. Some of the same conditions of economic crisis are there, and some of the same antipathies; in the competing claims of small and large farmer there is a marked element of class antagonism. And some of the same catch-cries are there – socialism, communism, fascism, 'the church in danger'.

But above all it was a round in an Irish struggle, and its ending was a part of an Irish anti-climax. The corporativists left no enduring heritage, and Fine Gael lost ground in the struggle to maintain an effective constitutional alternative to Fianna Fáil. But equally, as the thirties wore on, Fianna Fáil in turn slowly lost its emotional links with the I.R.A., and the I.R.A. itself, so far from being locked in a final struggle with either imperialism or fascism, saw its dream of a thirty-two county, and to many of its members, socialist republic dwindle into the futility of the suitcase bombings. In retrospect, the violence of the period is not surprising; given the great hopes and great fears of the contestants, it is more surprising that there was so little of it. Ten years after the civil war the Irish state was taking shape as a twenty-six county semi-republic, half in and half out of the Commonwealth, politically adjusted to parliamentary democracy, economically reconciled to private enterprise. In that shape it was, broadly speaking, to remain. For better or worse, the Irish people were jaded with political excitement, no matter from what source it came.

LABOUR AND THE POLITICAL REVOLUTION

Donal Nevin

Can the failure of the Labour Party to win a leading place in Irish political life after the Treaty be ascribed to the inadequacies of its leaders and defects of policy or was its weak position inevitable given the political circumstances that evolved from the Civil War?

The part played by James Connolly and the Irish Citizen Army in the Easter Rising ought to have given Labour title-deeds to a place in the leadership of the resurgent nation. The social radicalism of the Democratic Programme of the First Dáil might have seemed to underwrite Labour's basic philosophy. Labour, however, had stood aside at the 1918 elections in order that the people might declare themselves unambiguously on the question of self-determination. This self-abnegation on the part of Labour in the interests of national solidarity was to have profound implications for the future of the party. When the Treaty was signed, Labour stood aside from the ensuing controversy though, in effect, it accepted the Treaty. Its candidates at the 1922 elections had been left free to state their own position on the question of the Treaty but were pledged to attend and take part in the activities of whatever Parliament was set up.

An enduring legacy of the Civil War was the deep division between those who accepted the Treaty and those who opposed it. So long as this issue dominated politics, the influence of the Labour Party was bound to be marginal. Its potential influence was also affected by the partition of the country since an industrial working class existed mainly in the Belfast area. Thus the political division between north and south and the preoccupation with the issues of the Civil War within the Free State, were bound to affect adversely the size and influence of the Labour Party.

In the early years of the Free State, Labour was the sole

parliamentary opposition to the Cumann na nGaedheal Government. In this role it was assiduous and conscientious. The abstention of the elected Republican deputies, however, created extreme difficulties for the Labour opposition. The rejection by Mr. de Valera and his followers of the legitimacy of the Dáil in which the Labour deputies had taken their seats, estranged many Republicans whose social outlook would have made them natural allies of Labour.

The results of the general election held in June 1927 were distinctly favourable to Labour. Twenty-two Labour deputies were elected as compared with 14 in the outgoing Dáil. This compared with 44 for the recently-formed but still abstentionist party, Fianna Fáil and 47 for Cumann na nGaedheal. In some measure, Labour's good showing in this election could be ascribed to dissatisfaction at the abstention policy of Fianna Fáil. Many of the electors saw little point in electing to Parliament candidates who were pledged not to take their seats if elected and Labour certainly benefitted from this. Apart from this Labour had fought the election with a constructive programme on social and economic issues.

Two months after the election a new political situation was created with the entry of Fianna Fáil into the Dáil. Labour's role in the Dáil had been a relatively simple and straight-forward one. While in definite opposition to the Government it had voted according to the merits of each proposal that arose. It had moved votes of censure and votes of 'no confidence' on many occasions but on all these occasions, the party knew they were in a minority and could not succeed. Now an opportunity presented itself which could result in overthrowing the Government. As soon as the Fianna Fáil deputies had taken their seats, the Labour leader, Thomas Johnson, gave notice of a motion of 'no confidence'.

Much criticism was to be levelled at the Labour Party for its part in the political manoeuvring that followed. The National Executive of the Irish Labour Party and Trade Union Congress had considered what course of action the Parliamentary Labour Party should take if the Government were defeated and had decided that Labour should endeavour to form a government in co-operation with members of other parties excluding Cumann na nGaedheal and Fianna Fáil, on the understanding that the non-Labour elements, that is, Captain Redmond's National League and the Farmers, would not be allowed to dictate terms. Fianna Fáil, it was understood, would support such a Government.

The basis of the party's decision was that the best interests of the country would be served if for a time neither of the two evenly-balanced parties, which were in such bitter enmity, were maintained in power. Naively, perhaps, they saw this move as a means of assuaging the political passions arising from the Civil War. In the event, the result of the division on Labour's motion of 'no confidence' was a tie. A member of the National League, Alderman John Jinks, who had agreed to vote for the motion, had absented himself from the division. The Ceann Comhairle gave his casting vote against the motion and the Government was saved. Labour was not to be put to the test of forming a minority Government.

In the general election which followed shortly afterwards, Labour's fortunes slumped. Its vote dropped from 143,000 to 106,000. It suffered a net loss of nine seats and its representation was reduced to 13 deputies. The leader of the party, Thomas Johnson was defeated in County Dublin and William O'Brien, the general secretary of the Irish Transport and General Workers' Union, in Tipperary. The only consolation for Labour lay in the fact that the other small parties had fared worse. Both Cumann na nGaedheal and Fianna Fáil had increased their strength at the expense of the smaller parties. Here was a disquieting portent for Labour's hopes of becoming one of two main parties.

The loss of Thomas Johnson as leader of the party in the Dáil was severely felt by Labour. He was an outstandingly able parliamentarian, an opposition in himself, Stephen Gwynn declared. In Parliament his knowledge and judgment were invaluable to the party while his integrity was absolute and his capacity for work unlimited.

Under its new leader, T.J. O'Connell, the Labour Party during the remaining years of the nineteen twenties, became increasingly critical of the Cumann na nGaedheal Government for its failure to deal with worsening unemployment and the appalling housing conditions and for its reactionary attitude to social services. More often than not Labour deputies were to be found in the same lobby as Fianna Fáil though not always for the same reasons.

Meanwhile, attention was being given to the organisation and structure of the Labour and Trade Union Movement. Since 1918 there had been a single organisation, the Irish Labour Party and Trade Union Congress which combined industrial and political functions in a way that was probably unique among the Labour Movements of the world. In 1930 the industrial and political sides of the Movement separated into two independent and autonomous bodies, one the Irish T.U.C. and the other, the Irish Labour Party. One of the main purposes of the separation was to secure better organisation on the political side. Apart from a few constituencies there was no effective Labour organisation permanently in existence and it was thought that the weak representation of Labour in the Dáil was due to this fact. It cannot be said, however, that the change made in 1930 materially affected Labour organisation which remained weak and in the majority of constituencies virtually non-existent. The exceptions were those constituencies in which prominent local Labour figures had built up personal electoral machines. Many of the Labour deputies were to owe their election more to their own personal popularity than to the acceptance by their constituents of Labour policy and principles.

The trade union movement itself was going through a period of difficulty and disunity. Its membership had declined sharply during the nineteen twenties. Strong pressure by employers for a reduction in wages was to culminate in a big lock-out of building workers in the spring of 1931. Long-existing divisions in the movement were becoming more serious. Differences between competing Irish unions and British-based unions and other inter-union disputes flared up from time to time causing disunity and bitterness among trade union leaders. Excluded from the official fold was the militant Workers' Union of Ireland which had

58

been founded by Jim Larkin following his dispute with the Irish Transport and General Workers' Union.

The relations between the Labour Party and the Trade Union Movement remained close. The more important unions including the Irish Transport and General Workers' Union, were affiliated to the Party and delegates from unions constituted the great majority of the delegates at the annual party conference. Contrary to what may be supposed, the close association of the trade unions with the Labour Party did not provide the latter with the financial resources necessary to maintain an effective political organisation in the constituencies. While the Irish Transport Union in particular provided financial backing at elections to the candidates it sponsored, little money was forthcoming from the unions for the party as such, whether for organising purposes or for publicity and propaganda. The daily press was unsympathetic to Labour yet the Movement found great difficulty in maintaining its own organ. For five years up to the end of 1932, the Irish T.U.C. published a weekly paper called *The Irishman,* later renamed, *The Watchword* but neither under the editorship of R.J.P. Mortished nor Cathal O'Shannon did it have a significant circulation.

The first test of the separate political organisation, the Irish Labour Party, came in the general election held in 1932. It entered the election campaign with its parliamentary ranks reduced to 10 by two expulsions and one death. In 1931, Daniel Morrissey and Richard Anthony had been expelled from the party for voting with Cumann na nGaedheal for a drastic public safety bill setting up a Military Tribunal which had been strongly opposed by the Labour Party. Mr. Morrissey subsequently was to join Fine Gael while Mr. Anthony re-joined the Labour Party.

Though the Labour vote in the 1932 election declined only slightly as compared with September 1927, the party won only seven seats. Five outgoing deputies were defeated including the party leader, Mr. O'Connell. Fianna Fáil with 72 seats was the largest party in the Dáil but short of a majority. Labour with its seven seats held the balance of power. It was clear that Labour would give its support to Fianna Fáil. The party was determined, however, to maintain its position of complete independence and had decided that it would neither seek nor accept office in the new Government to which it would give general support where the measures introduced were not in conflict with the policy of the Labour Party.

It was William Norton, the new leader of the party, who was to speak in support of the nomination of Mr. de Valera as President of the Executive Council. Mr. Norton, the general secretary of the Post Office Workers' Union, was young, able, shrewd and an effective platform speaker. He had first been returned to the Dáil in a by-election in 1926 but had lost his seat in the following year. He was to emerge as an astute parliamentary figure and, for a period, was to lead the Labour Party to the left.

In his speech supporting Mr. de Valera, Mr. Norton was forthright in his condemnation of the Cumann na nGaedheal regime and in his call for radical departures in economic policy. 'In the struggle for freedom' Mr. Norton said, 'the workers of Ireland did not join merely for the purpose of exchanging one capitalist system for another. For ten years the Labour Party had pleaded with Cumann na nGaedheal to remember the Democratic Programme of the First Dáil and the pledges given to the workers by Sinn Féin. We have pleaded in vain. Now they are on the eve of going out of office and having regard to their record towards the workers there will be no tears shed and no regrets expressed. Fianna Fáil at least promises that it will tackle the social and economic problems pressing with so much rigour on the workers. It is because we in the Labour Party have hopes that Fianna Fáil will live up to their declared policy that we were going to vote for Deputy de Valera.'

It is unlikely that William Norton believed that Fianna Fáil was likely to replace the capitalist system. The leader of that party, however, was at pains to emphasise his acceptance of Labour aspirations and indeed professed to seeing no basic difference in the policies of Fianna Fáil and Labour. Shortly after the general election, Mr. de Valera was to declare with passion that the thing that was most heartbreaking to him since he came into the Dáil was to find Fianna Fáil and Labour, who should have stood side by side, divided, adding that the two parties had the same programme. 'I never regarded freedom as an end in itself', Mr. de Valera told the Dáil 'but if I were asked what statement of Irish policy was most in accord with my view as to what human beings should struggle for, I would stand side by side with James Connolly'.

Throughout 1932 Labour gave full though not uncritical support to the Fianna Fáil Government. Many of its social measures, notably in the field of housing, were in line with long-standing Labour policy. Its fiscal policy as reflected in the 1932 Budget, when the standard rate of income tax was raised from 3/6d to 5/-d in the £, accorded with Labour's thinking. While supporting in general the policy of tariff protection as a means of developing industry, Labour was sceptical of the Government's industrial programme. Capitalism plus tariffs would not solve the country's problems, Mr. Norton said. Labour was critical too of Fianna Fáil's handling of the land annuities dispute but when the British Government imposed duties on Irish agricultural produce in retaliation for the withholding of the land annuities, Labour immediately declared that the British Government had challenged the Irish people on a political as well as an economic issue. The question it said was one of subjugation or independence, equality or subordination. The Labour Party availed themselves of this opportunity to press the Government to make radical changes in the economy since temporary adjustments would be utterly futile. 'The alternative to surrendering to Cumann na nGaedheal, now more reactionary than ever,' Labour declared, 'and leaving them to make the best terms with the British Government, was to pursue a determined policy of rapid reconstruction of the economic system based on the principles of the 1916 Proclamation and the Democratic Programme of 1919.' Labour sought to push Fianna Fáil to the left.

At the 1933 election Labour defended its policy of supporting Mr. de Valera but the verdict was inconclusive so far as Labour was concerned. Though the Labour vote fell, it gained one seat, increasing its representation to eight deputies.

Developments among the opposition parties were soon however to bring Labour and Fianna Fáil closer together. When in September 1933, Cumann na nGaedheal combined with the Centre Party to form the new United Ireland or Fine Gael party, under the leadership of General Eoin O'Duffy, negotiations took place between the Labour Party and the Government. As a result an arrangement was arrived at under which the Government undertook to give effect to a number of important planks in Labour's programme. Widows' pensions were to be introduced as well as unemployment assistance; improvements in the workmen's compensation code and a new conditions of employment act were promised and the housing programme was to be speeded up. It was also agreed that there would be regular meetings between the Labour Party and the Government and that the Labour Party was to be consulted in advance on all projected legislation.

It was not so much these concessions to Labour that impelled it to draw closer to the Government as the growing threat of Fascism. On 2nd August 1933, Mr. Norton referring to the setting up of General O'Duffy's National Guard modelled, as he put it, on the best Hitlerite lines, had said that Labour would fight in the most uncompromising manner any attempt to destroy the democratic political institutions of the State. The Trade Unions saw behind the Blueshirt Movement the hope of reactionary politicians that they could exploit economic distress and ride to power in the storm, as the President of the Irish Trade Union Congress put is. Trade union leaders, alerted by what had happened in Italy and Germany were alarmed at the statements being made by the leaders of the United Ireland Party. A joint manifesto was issued by the Irish T.U.C. and the Labour Party and a campaign of demonstrations organised throughout the country.

The manifesto declared that the pronouncements of Fascist advocates, some of them prominent men in the political life of the country, constituted a grave danger to the free existence of trade unions as well as pointing to the overthrow of democratic government. In this attack on the principles of democracy and trade unionism, the forces of landlordism and reaction were becoming linked with disappointed party politicians avaricious for power under Fascist leadership, portending the gravest menace the workers had ever been called on to face. The issue was one of life and death for democracy and trade unionism. The threat may have been exaggerated but the Labour and Trade Union leaders were genuinely alarmed at the development of the Blueshirt Movement and the threat of a Corporate State.

Suggestions for a united front against Fascism were made by a new organisation, the Republican Congress, which had been organised by a section of the I.R.A. headed by Frank Ryan and Peadar O'Donnell. Over the years there had been very little contact between Labour and the extreme Republicans some of whom held advanced views on social issues. The implicitly pro-Treaty and fundamentally conservative attitude of the majority of the Labour leaders had inhibited any collaboration between them and when in October 1934 a motion came before the Labour Party conference calling for a united front with the Republican Congress it won little support and was easily defeated. Subsequently some of those associated with the Republican Congress, notably Michael Price, joined the Labour Party.

With the disintegration of the Blueshirt Movement, relations between the Labour Party and the Government became less close. The Labour Party complained that Fianna Fáil was turning away from the programme it had set out prior to taking office and that in matters affecting social relations it was adhering to the conservative practice of their predecessors. Disillusionment with the high promise of Fianna Fáil's coming to power was soon to change into active opposition to that party.

Labour itself continued to move left. Though deriving its basic philosophy and outlook from the teachings of James Connolly, the party never called itself a socialist party and in this differed from the British Labour Party, for example. True it was anti-capitalist. Its constitution adopted in 1930 comdemned 'the social system inherited by the present generation as anti-national and non-moral'. In its place the party proposed vaguely the organisation of agriculture and industry on co-operative lines and public control of banking and transport. A proposal to include in the constitution as an objective of the party the winning for the workers of Ireland collectively, the ownership and control of the whole produce of their labour was defeated. At the time, William McMullen criticised the party's objects as 'pale pink, bourgeois objects that anybody could subscribe to' while Cathal O'Shannon pleaded with the party to 'pitch its banner a little nearer to the skies'. Symbolically perhaps, the *Red Flag* which had been sung at the conclusion of annual conferences during the twenties was replaced by the *Watchword of Labour*.

From 1932 onwards, however, the party adopted a more radical position. In his addresses as chairman of the Labour Party, a position he held from 1933 to 1938, William O'Brien, a key figure in the trade union and in the political movement spoke of the world collapse of capitalism, the complete failure of private enterprise to serve the needs of the people and the necessity for breaking the stranglehold of the private banking system. Mr. Norton spoke of the need for economic planning and a National Economic Council. In 1934 the general secretary of the party Luke Duffy, moved a motion declaring that it was the aim of the Labour Party to continue Connolly's efforts for the establishment in Ireland of a Workers' Republic.

The new constitution adopted by the Labour Party early in 1936 was to consolidate this shift to the left. Not only did it incorporate as an objective the proposal rejected in 1930 but it also proclaimed as an objective 'the establishment in Ireland of a Workers' Republic founded on the principles of social justice, sustained by democratic institutions and guaranteeing civil and religious liberty and equal opportunities to achieve happiness to all citizens who render service to the community'. It was the leader of the party, Mr. Norton who proposed the new programme to the party conference. 'This is the portion of our programme which will be most bitterly assailed by the imperialist elements in the country', he declared, 'but Labour makes no apology for declaring in favour in a Workers'

64

Republic', adding meaningfully, that those who remembered the concepts of freedom for which Connolly worked and dreamed, would understand the setting-down of that objective.

The term 'Workers' Republic' had a history long associated with Labour in Ireland and was probably peculiar to Ireland. It was the title given to the weekly organ of the Irish Socialist Republican Party established by James Connolly in 1898 and was again used by him for the paper he edited in 1915 and 1916. The Workers' Republic was in fact set as the objective of the Irish Labour Party and T.U.C. in its address to the Workers of Ireland in 1922 immediately following the Dáil decision on the Treaty.

Yet within three years, the party constitution was to be amended and the Workers' Republic removed. The change arose out of a lengthy correspondence between one of the trade unions affiliated to the party and the Hierarchy which culminated in the Hierarchy expressing its objection to the aim of the party being a Workers' Republic. It fell to Mr. Norton to propose that the constitution be changed.

'The Labour Party is a political party', he told the delegates, 'and objection has been taken by the Hierarchy to the term, Workers' Republic. If the conference wants to avoid the deliberate misrepresentations which opponents would employ against us, it is necessary to delete the term from the Constitution. Conference will have to make up its mind whether it is not wiser for the party to drop the term.' The conference, by 89 votes to 25, agreed that it was wiser to do so.

Growing disenchantment with Fianna Fáil was evident in Labour's programme for the 1937 general election. It warned the people that only by the presence of an effective Labour Party in the Dáil would legislation be enacted to effect the reforms necessary to achieve social justice. Their experience of both Cumann na nGaedheal and Fianna Fáil should be a warning that neither could be relied upon willingly to carry through the Dáil essential measures of social reform.

The results of the election represented a significant advance for Labour. While the Fianna Fáil and the Fine Gael vote each dropped by nearly 90,000, the Labour vote increased by 56,000 or by more than two-thirds. The party secured 13 seats in a House of 138 members as against the eight seats won in 1933 in a House of 153 members. For the third and last time the Labour deputies voted for Mr. de Valera's election as head of the government.

Within a year there was another election. A motion calling for the establishment of arbitration machinery for the Civil Service was supported by Labour and in the absence of fourteen Fianna Fáil deputies in the critical division, the Government was defeated. At this election Labour strongly criticised the dictatorial tendencies of the Government and the attempt to stampede the electorate to return a majority of yes-men amenable to the pressure of party interests with a dictatorial executive and a subservient Parliament as the Fianna Fáil conception of representative Government. Though the decline in the overall Labour vote was fractional, the party returned only nine deputies as compared with thirteen in 1937.

Thus after six elections over little more than a decade, Labour in 1938 held only 9 seats in the Dáil as compared with 22 following the election in the summer of 1927. Over nearly half this period it had opposed a Cumann na nGaedheal government while over the second half it had pretty steadfastly supported the government of Fianna Fáil. While it could claim to have exercised some influence in respect of the progressive social measures introduced by Mr. de Valera's government in its early years of office, its overall political influence remained marginal. It showed few signs of becoming an alternative government. Indeed, it had no illusions as to the likelihood even of its displacing either of the two main parties. The most it could hope for was to hold the balance between them and thereby exert an influence on policy disproportionate to its size. In the circumstances of the time, with the political passions generated by the Civil War still close to the surface and with many of the outstanding personalities of the sundered national independence movement still holding leading positions in the main parties, it was probably inevitable that Labour should play a minor role.

66

One of the paradoxes of Labour's situation was that while it represented the political arm of the trade unions, it drew its main electoral support from predominately rural constituencies and that in Dublin, with its concentration of trade union members, it commanded negligible support. Loyalties born of the Civil War divisions proved stronger than any class consciousness or any disposition to follow the political promptings of the trade union movement.

The image of the party among the public at large was one of a party that stood for social reform but was not quite sure as to how it should be achieved; a party that sought basic changes in the structure of the economy and of society yet was extremely sensitive to charges of being too radical. Because of its attitude to the Treaty and the conservative views on the national question held by some of its leading figures, Labour provided no strong appeal for republicans. To many supporters of Fianna Fáil, Labour had committed the error of anticipating Mr. de Valera by five years and taking their seats in the Dáil in 1922 rather than in 1927. Its timidity alienated many of the intellectuals who from time to time drifted into the party and who soon drifted out again. Being a small party it could not benefit from the bandwagon impulse as did the larger parties. It became a victim of its smallness which was one of its greatest handicaps in presenting itself to the electorate. Being small it found it difficult to develop an effective political organisation which in turn limited its prospects of electoral success. How to break out of this vicious circle was the problem confronting the party as the nineteen 'thirties drew to a close.

Nevertheless, the very fact of the existence of the Labour Party, however weak and ineffectual it might have appeared, profoundly influenced the attitude of the other parties to social issues. Its constant stress on these issues, and its policies on them, contributed to a greater awareness and understanding of them. Throughout the period from 1927 to the end of the 'thirties the Labour Party was well in advance of opinion in the other parties on such questions as the importance of public enterprise for the development of the economy and the necessity for economic planning.

It consistently urged the need for comprehensive and co-ordinated social services and equality of opportunity in education. Increasingly, it was to find portions of its programme taken up by other parties and as this happened the distinctiveness of Labour's policy became less clear and ironically, the party had to face the charge that there was no fundamental difference between it and these other parties.

FROM FREE TRADE TO SELF-SUFFICIENCY

Professor James Meenan

In the year 1926 the Irish Free State was a free trading country, which had indeed imposed some protective tariffs but was still in general led by the principles of economic orthodoxy. Ten years later its protective tariff was as high as any country in the world; and its policies tended towards the goal of self-sufficiency. There was nothing exceptional in this. The same swing of policy may be seen in many other countries at the time. But with us, the swing was particularly violent, and economics and politics were inextricably mixed up together. Years before, Sir Horace Plunkett had remarked that in Ireland, political economy was spelled with a large 'P' and a small 'e'. His words could be applied with justice to the years between 1926 and 1936.

In 1926 the Cumann na nGaedheal government was already four years in office. Its economic policy had been fully thought out. It was a policy which leant against protection, in industry as well as in agriculture. There might, it was agreed be a case to be made for industrial protection, but the onus of proof rested on those who asked for a tariff.

Some tariffs, indeed, had already been applied. The very first formal budget of the Irish Free State, in April 1924, had imposed a number, on commodities such as boots and shoes, confectionery, and soap and candles. Further protective duties followed in 1925 and 1926. These decisions were taken with caution and after examination of the merits of each case. The government, as Mr. Ernest Blythe (then Minister for Finance) declared had no doctrinaire attitude on the question of free trade and protection. It regarded the matter as one of expediency which might be variously decided in different circumstances. It was one on which the country should feel its way.

A Tariff Commission was therefore appointed in 1926

to examine applications for protection by tariff. It discharged its duties carefully, meticulously and – according to ardent protectionists – appallingly slowly. In the event, between 1924 and the depression year of 1931, rather more than a dozen duties were imposed. These duties related to industries that were already established and that gave promise of growth. Those conditions limited the field considerably; and we must always remember that the established major industries of the time – which in practice meant brewing and distilling – had no desire for protection at all. Further, for reasons that we will see in a moment, there was no protection for agricultural produce at all, if the exceptional case of sugar-beet, whose origins belong to this period, is excluded.

This was a curious turn-about for a Cumann na nGaedheal government. After all they were in office as the defenders of the Treaty settlement of 1921. Arthur Griffith had been the leader of the delegation that signed that Treaty. His whole lifework, summed up in his book *The Resurrection of Hungary,* had been to preach the gospel of tariff protection for infant industries. It was generally understood that he had never troubled much about the precise trappings of self-government, whether royal or republican, as long as it included the one vital power – the power to impose tariffs. Here then, were his political heirs in power; and they disregarded his economic testament. Why was this?

An answer was given in the Dail during a typically uncompromising speech by Kevin O'Higgins. 'The propagandist writings of any one man cannot be accepted simply as revealed truth, requiring no further investigation, something that must be accepted for ever as beyond question, beyond doubt, beyond the need of examination.'

The fact was that the first government was convinced beyond question or doubt, of the need to give its first attention to agriculture. At that time of the 1920's it must be remembered, over fifty per cent of the working population were engaged in agriculture; nearly two-thirds of the total population lived outside towns. The greater part of the national income (not then precisely calculated) came from agriculture. Obviously then, the first thing for a government to do was to make agriculture prosperous. Once it was prosperous, then the benefits would filter through to everybody else in the country to the small industrialists, the shop-keepers, the professions.

But it was clear that farmers could be prosperous only if they were able to export, granted the small size of the home market. To export meant to sell in the British market where at that time there were no tariffs against any country. But precisely because the British market was open to the world, the Irish farmer had to compete against Danish and New Zealand butter, Polish and Chinese eggs. He could only do so if his products were of good quality and capable of being sold at a competitive price.

The first government therefore aimed at two things. First, to improve the standard of Irish farm products. This was done by means of a succession of Acts regulating breeding of livestock, and the quality of dairy produce. They were regarded as almost totalitarian at the time; and indeed it was the first time in this country that the power of the State had been used to impose standards of production and marketing.

The second point went much further. Farmers had to sell in a foreign and fiercely competitive market. They could only do so if they could produce as cheaply as possible. Therefore, they should be able to buy whatever they needed as cheaply as possible. In this view it was preferable to import maize rather than to produce homegrown feeding stuffs. It was preferable to import wheat rather than to sacrifice land to growing it at home. Irish farming, in other words, was to be geared to the export market; it was not to be protected in its own market.

In the same way, tariffs for industry should be imposed only with the greatest care, so that farmers should not pay more than they should. That ruled out an allround tariff. Similarly, rates and taxes were to be kept as low as possible. And so, by the end of the 1920's income tax stood at 3/6d. in the pound. But that was achieved only by extreme prudence in public expenditure, which meant that social expenditure was heavily limited.

This then was a policy which gave priority to the farmers. They were not unduly grateful. Oliver Gogarty remarked at the time that the Farmers' Party existed in order to oppose everything. That may have been unfair, although they were among the foremost opponents of the Shannon Scheme in 1924-25; but there was an element of truth in it. The spirit in which the new standards were enforced did not attract immediate support. Priority to agriculture is of course inseparably associated with the name of Patrick Hogan who was Minister for Agriculture until 1932. He defined his policy once as 'helping the farmer who helped himself and letting the rest go to the devil.' One way or another this policy antagonised a lot of people – many farmers; all protectionists, not to mention old age pensioners and civil servants who found their pensions or salaries reduced as the cost of living fell.

Nevertheless an observer of these policies in 1931 might well have decided that they had been highly successful. Even in industry the number in employment had grown from 103 thousand in 1926 to 111 thousand in 1931. Irish agricultural produce regained its place in the British market. These, it must be remembered, were still the days in which we sold butter and eggs freely and without subsidy. In 1929 both products enjoyed top prices in that competitive market. But the most striking point is made by looking at the export figure for that year of 1929. It was valued at £47 million – a figure which was not again approached until 1948, by which time of course the pounds were worth far less. There is another comparison, the volume of exports in 1929 was not exceeded in any subsequent year until as lately as 1960. Lastly, in 1929 the value of exports was 77 per cent. of the value of imports, a ratio which we have never managed to approach since then except during the war years when imports were hard to find.

October of that year, 1929, brought the collapse on the New York stock exchange which brought in the Great Depression. Thereafter prices fell all over the world in industry and in agriculture while unemployment rose. In September 1931 Great Britain was forced off the Gold Standard. Its new government, the National Government which received an enormous majority in the general election of October 1931, announced its intention of imposing a tariff, the first general British tariff since the 1850's, and of protecting British agriculture. The export market was not gone – Irish products would have been eligible for preferential treatment; but quite clearly it would not be what it had been in the free-trading twenties. The assumptions on which Hogan's policy was based would need revision.

But there was a great deal more involved than a change of tariff policy. There was a world-wide revulsion from the old orthodoxies which had been accepted in the 1920's. In 1931 and 1932 it seemed to many people that the depression might well go on forever, and that the exchange economy based on international trade and low tariffs had irretrievably broken down. The collapse of the Gold Standard seemed to be the end of an era. This mood was to be found everywhere. It intensified the forces making for high protection (and ultimately for full State control) in countries such as Germany and Italy. Even the United States increased its already high tariff. And the end was clearly come when even Great Britain, whose nineteenth century prosperity had been founded on free trade, turned to the protection of a tariff wall.

In this country, of course, the nationalist tradition had always favoured protection. It was taken for granted, before the Treaty, that self-government would lead at once to tariffs on foreign goods entering the country. It seemed self-evident that if industry and agriculture were protected, the unending emigration would be brought under control. If our supply of wheat were grown at home instead of being imported, if every kind of tillage were encouraged, work on the farms would be found for those who emigrated. If manufactures received the advantage of a tariff against foreign goods, then work would be found in the towns for those who came off the farms. All this seemed too evident to need discussion. Griffith, as I have said, set the argument on its legs in his *Resurrection of Hungary*.

But there was something deeper still, which indeed will be found in Griffith although it was not essential to his argument as he put it. It was not simply that a country that depended on agriculture alone was like a man with only one arm. It was rather that such a country was socially and spiritually the poorer. It was rather a feeling that a country in which the principal products were cattle, brewing and distilling would be a country where there was little opportunity or variety in life, lacking skill and enterprise and change, all the qualities that give life to a country. I can best illustrate this often half-conscious feeling by quoting A.E. – who was certainly neither a doctrinaire protectionist nor a follower of the political party which advocated all-round protection.

Writing in the *Irish Statesman,* as early as 1925, he noted that the case for protection was 'not so much an economic case as an intellectual and cultural case. If the country lives almost altogether by a few industries its intellectual life will lack richness and variety, and our cultural life has lacked richness and depth because agriculture... did not find employment for large numbers of engineers, electricians, chemists and bacteriologists.'

That was an intellectual view. There was also a political view. The Fianna Fáil party was founded in 1926. It combined opposition to Griffith's political settlement with advocacy of his economic teaching. As early as February 1928, six months after the party had entered the Dáil, Mr. Lemass moved a resolution declaring that the Tariff Commission was not sufficiently expeditious in its examination of applications for tariff protection. A short extract from his speech on that occasion might be quoted. 'We believe' he said 'that Ireland can be made a selfcontained unit, providing all the necessities of living in adequate quantities for the people residing in the island at the moment and probably for a much larger number.'

That claim, it will be noticed, went far beyond a policy of protection. Griffith had advocated tariffs for the same reasons as his master, the German economist, List. Protection was to be given to infant industries in their early years. It was to be removed when they had become strong enough to meet competition. That is to say, the continuance of international trade was taken for granted. There was no suggestion of self-sufficiency.

Therefore, the long debates on economic policy which occupied the Dáil between 1928 and 1932 were fruitless. It was not simply that the Fianna Fáil opposition were more in favour of tariffs than the Cumann na nGaedheal government. The dividing line became more and more whether one favoured self-sufficiency or not, which was an issue which went far beyond a matter of economics because it obviously depended on what kind of Ireland was hoped for. The two sides were not arguing about the same things.

The full protectionist case advanced slowly as long as world prosperity lasted. It leaped ahead with the spread of the great depression. When Fianna Fáil formed their first government in March, 1932 they introduced tariffs all round. Their first budget, in May, contained forty-three new duties. One observer wrote that 'if a Glasgow communist and a die-hard tariff reformer were merged into a single personality and, having somehow managed to escape certification, became Minister for Finance in the Irish Free State, the result would probably be something similar to the budget introduced in the Dáil...' The Minister concerned – it may surprise some thirty years after, – was Mr. MacEntee.

In industry, therefore, the change was complete. Tariffs were imposed as and when they were needed, not always with prior consultation with the interests concerned. This, it might be said, was inevitable. The interests concerned were often import agents: they took some time to realise the opportunities offered to them by the imposition of a tariff. The trend towards protection was, of course, intensified by the outbreak of the annuity dispute in the summer of 1932.

This affected agriculture directly. But here we are concerned with long-term policy rather than with the reactions to the penal British duties on Irish farm products entering Great Britain. That policy was based on the assumption that international trade of the type known in the 1920's could no longer be depended on. There would never again be an export market accessible. Therefore it was necessary to produce at home everything that could be grown here. There would still be agricultural exports (and indeed there would always be some surplus for export unless half the countryside was to be abandoned); but they were to be the residuals of production, not the prime end. In future farm exports were to serve the end of paying for the necessary imports of raw materials for industry and of the commodities which could not be produced at all in this country.

All this is set out very clearly in the evidence given to the Banking Commission which was appointed in 1934. Agricultural self-sufficiency was to be sought under four main headings, one at least of which may now raise an eyebrow. There was to be an expansion in the home production of, first wheat and feeding stuffs, second, of fruit such as apples and soft fruits; third, of vegetables, fourth, of tobacco production. Thus existing imports would be saved. Further, there was to be an energetic drive to find new markets. Lastly, and of greatest importance, there would be a gradual run-down of the number of cattle. Let us see how far these aims were achieved.

The vigorous encouragement of tillage took the form of providing minimum prices for home-grown wheat, the difference between them and world prices being made good out of public funds. A proportion of home-grown grain was to be mixed with all maize meal for animal food. Imports of sugar and of tobacco were controlled and the duties reduced in order to encourage domestic production.

As for foreign markets, the early 1930's were not years in which new channels of international trade could be easily constructed; and the search for them proved almost completely unsuccessful. Possible opportunities were limited by the fact that the prospective purchasers were uncertain payers. The most important trade agreement was that concluded with Germany. It provided that the Germans would buy one pound worth of Irish goods in return for our buying three pounds worth of theirs. Progress along those lines was not encouraging.

Exports were encouraged by bounties on exports of live cattle, butter, bacon and eggs, horses and dead poultry. As almost all these products went to Great Britain, this measure may have seemed illogical to those who will spoke of starving John Bull into surrender; but it was the most obvious common sense to give farmers some source of remuneration.

The decision to reduce cattle herds was implemented in 1934 by the provision of a bounty on calf-skins and of a scheme for the free distribution of beef to the unemployed. This was the one part of the new policy which might have had really important consequences; but the slaughter of the calves was plainly so severe a shock to public opinion that the scheme had a short life. Not many months later, in January 1935, the first of what were known as the Coal-Cattle pacts was agreed on between the British and Irish governments. This was not a sign that the quarrel over the annuities had been composed – that did not happen until the Anglo-Irish agreements of April 1938. It was not even a suspension of economic hostilities, because both the British coal entering Ireland and the Irish cattle entering Britain were subject to the penal duties imposed by each government. But it was very rightly regarded as a sign that neither government was prepared to press its policy too far. In the last resort, the British government would once again accept imports from Ireland and the Irish government was prepared to benefit by access to the export market. That was the end of self-sufficiency – until the war brought it to us in earnest.

But in fact, when one looks at it, the policies followed in the years just after 1932 were not policies of self-sufficiency, however they might have been described at the time. The industrial tariffs were imposed on finished goods entering the country. It was accepted that the new industries would flourish by processing or assembling imported raw materials. Only here and there were native sources of supply developed; and that could be done only slowly and with considerable expense. But if the raw materials had to be brought in, they had to be paid for and in the last resort they could be paid for only by exports. The country could not retire into isolation, even if several members of the government would have accepted isolation without regret.

In the same way, the new agricultural policy was not at all so revolutionary as both its supporters and its antagonists claimed. If it had been fully successful, it would have meant an increase of tillage of the order of about 1,200,000 acres over the 1931 level. That would have been substantial but not so very important when set against a total of 17 million acres of agricultural land. The Banking Commission obtained agreement on the estimate that the diversion of land from pasture would have been of the order of 10 to 13 per cent., a change certainly but not a revolution. In the same way, the saving of imports from the development of wheat-growing and the rest would have meant a saving of about five million pounds a year. That sum then represented ten per cent of all imports and just equalled the annual export of stout.

What then was the change between 1931 and 1936? Industrial employment rose sharply from 111 thousand in 1931 to 154 thousand in 1936; and the increase was almost entirely in manufacturing industry. In agriculture, the area under wheat rose from a derisory 2 thousand acres in 1931, the last summer of free trade, to 255 thousand acres in 1936. This, however, was largely achieved by changing out of other crops; and the total tillage area rose only from 1,425 thousand acres in 1931 to 1,621 thousand acres in 1936. Even the cattle herd, which had taken the full brunt of the annuities dispute, showed little change between the beginning and the end of the period. It numbered 4,029 thousand in 1931 and 4,014 thousand in 1936. The export trade indeed showed its scars. Exports were valued at £36 millions in 1931. They fell to just under £18 millions in the appalling year of 1934. In 1936 they were £22½ million. Perhaps the greatest lesson to learn from such figures is that, barring outright revolution and changes of accepted ways of life, it is very difficult indeed to change any economy quickly.

And in conclusion – which policy was more suitable – free trade or protection? The question seems inevitable, but it may not be wise to ask it, still less to attempt to answer it. The circumstances of 1926 to 1931 differed so radically from those of 1932 to 1936 that comparison is almost impossible. The present speaker maintains his belief that the policies followed by Hogan and his colleagues were beyond any argument the policies best fitted to the times in which they held office. He must equally confess that, if Hogan had been returned to office in 1932 some revision of his policies would have been inevitable. He would, one is sure, have held firmly to the most precious part of his policy, the insistence on efficiency of production and marketing, and regularity of supply. To-day we are still paying the price for the prolonged neglect of export markets – however inevitable that might have been in the 1940's.

But one must also say that in the circumstances of the great depression, it was necessary for any government to maintain, even to invent, employment at any cost. Ireland did not suffer the mass unemployment that was known to Britain, the United States and Germany. But emigration had dried up with the depression; indeed there were for some years more people returning from the States than were going there. It was not enough to preach, even to practice, the economic virtues and hope for the best. As Keynes said at the time, the maintenance of democracy depended on governments creating employment, no matter how uneconomic. But to leave it at that would be unfair. Eventually, out of the then unpromising tariff-created industries has come the pool of managerial experience and enterprise on which we rely so much to-day. And, in the last resort, energetic government policies at that time of crisis meant that the new Irish state succeeded in a task in which many much older-established nations then failed – in maintaining parliamentary government and the rule of law.

PUBLIC ADMINISTRATION 1927–36

T. J. Barrington

I

The newly independent Ireland of forty years ago contrasts strongly in the field of government with a newly independent African country of today. Ireland inherited a complete apparatus of government, both central and local. In 1923 21,000 civil servants transferred to the new State, of whom less than a thousand decided in the first few years not to continue to serve. At present time a newly independent African country of comparable population might have a civil service of some 2,000 people. Of these, all the senior and middle rank jobs would be filled by Europeans, most of whom are likely to have left the country within two or three years. In Ireland our public service had a solid basis of recruitment in well established universities and secondary schools. In the African country there may well be no university, and perhaps three or four secondary schools in the whole country giving the full range of secondary education. Thus, by contrast the African state would have a very undeveloped public service, virtually no trained public servants, and a wholly inadequate educational system to provide the considerable numbers of educated manpower and woman-power that would be needed. I make these points to stress that, whatever may have been the pains of independence in Ireland, we started off with an immense advantage in having well settled governmental institutions. There is both strength and weakness here. There is a striking passage in the report of the Brennan Commission of Enquiry into the Civil Service that sat from 1932 to 35. It says:

(8) 'The passing of the State services into the control of a native Government, however revolutionary it may have been as a step in the political development of

the nation, entails, broadly speaking, no immediate disturbance of any fundamental kind in the daily work of the average Civil Servant. Under changed masters the same main tasks of administration continue to be performed by the same staffs on the same general lines of organization and procedure...'

One can see the sense of this. For the man administering, let us say, the Diseases of Animals Acts, the fact of serving an Irish rather than a British Government did not alter the determination to ensure, for example, that foot and mouth disease was prevented.

But there is another side to this question. If there was no fundamental change in the business of government, what indeed had all the fuss been about? The core of the problem of public administration in Ireland during the 1920's and 1930's – and indeed for a long time afterwards – is the failure to resolve this paradox.

When we talk of government we think of two things. First, of course, of 'the Government' the political rulers of the country; but, secondly, of 'the business of government', the carrying on of the various state services. Public administration is concerned substantially with the second of these. It can be divided into four broad areas – central government, local government, functional government and appellate government. By central government we mean the kinds of services carried on by the civil service – say in the Department of Agriculture, or the Post Office or the Department of Finance. By local government we mean the road or health or housing services provided by local authorities. By functional government we mean the sorts of specialized services provided by the state agencies – whether it be the supply of electricity, or sugar, or the promotion of tourist development. By appellate government we mean the system that exists to resolve disputes that arise when decisions adversely affecting the individual are taken by the other forms of government. I propose to say a few words about each of these four areas of government during our period, and then to draw a few conclusions.

II

CENTRAL GOVERNMENT

First central government.
The Irish civil service had developed pari passu with the English civil service over a period of some seventy years from the beginning of reform in 1855 up to the granting of independence. Legislation in 1923 established the system of open competition for recruitment through the Civil Service Commission and in 1924 the setting up of government departments under a minister who was, legally, the only person in the department normally entitled to take decisions. The old system that had operated in Ireland whereby decision making was done by Boards of one kind or another was substantially abolished and the minister, as the corporation soul, emerged, with the department, in law, simply an extension of his personality. It was, of course, essential to ensure that the civil service would remain subordinate to political control; but the contrary danger does not seem to have been realised. This is that the civil service would remain *too* subordinate to exercise enough initiative to think up solutions for some at least of the great problems of the time. If all that was required was to carry on as before, as the extract I have quoted from the report of the Brennan Commission would seem to suggest, then subordination was an important issue; but if the civil service was to play an important part in a developing situation – and development was clearly necessary if the problems of the country, with its heavy emigration rate and loss of population, were to be solved – then something else was clearly required. The real issue became to try to discover, within the proper democratic framework, a means by which the dynamics of the public service could be harnessed to the development of the community. So far as one can see, either this issue was not recognised as an issue, or it was dodged.

Civil servants after the first World War were paid a basic salary with a cost of living bonus. During the 1920's and early 1930's the cost of living fell and the pay of civil servants fell accordingly. This led to some discontent. There was also discontent about failure to establish a proper means of resolving disputes between the staff and the Department of Finance. For these and other reasons a commission of enquiry, the Brennan Commission, was set up in 1932 and reported in 1935. The report itself shows a sensible appreciation of day to day problems, and suggests some useful tightening of bolts and nuts: but of awareness of the deep underlying issues the report reveals no evidence.

The most important of these issues is, of course, what are the springs of public policy in a free, democratic society? No doubt there are many of these, but, as recent experience has shown, one of the important sources of policy is the public service itself. This has long been recognised. One of the stated duties of the administrative class in the civil service, quoted by the Commission, is 'the formation of policy'.

In the 1920's the main aim of administration seems to have been the pursuit of 'efficiency' in the narrow sense – that is the avoidance of observable waste. For example, the civil service was both smaller and cheaper in 1934 than it had been in 1923. But economy of this kind is, at best, only a secondary aim. What was the primary aim? In the 1930's considerable administrative activity was devoted to the laying of the foundations of an industrial community, and in developing such welfare services as housing. The first of these came from the thinking of Sinn Féin some twenty years previously. The second came from the new climate of social compassion that gained momentum all through the 1930's. These were, however, forces that played on the administration from outside. There is no evidence that there was spontaneous growth of new and relevant policy formulation within the system of public administration itself.

It is clear that an important way of evoking new ideas and thinking is to free the human dynamics of the public organizations themselves. This can be done both by removing the impediments to, and by fostering the forces that stimulate, creative ideas. In civil service terms the impediments are substantially organizational. To simplify a far too elaborate grading structure, to rationalise the distribution of business, to concentrate responsibility as between different bodies, to modernize financial controls, to tease out the respective areas of responsibility between administrators and professional men – these are the big organizational issues of the civil service. Of the existence of these problems, the majority report betrays no real awareness. The Civil Service Clerical Association posed for them the problem of multiplicity of grades, and Mr. L.J. Duffy, in a minority report raised this and also the question of the orderly distribution of the business of government; but these representations had no observable effect. The positive forces, that encourage people to give of their best, are to use the incentive of promotion to creative ends, to train officials in the best discharge of their duties, to intellectualise officials at the highest levels, to stimulate research into economic and social problems. In the main report and in the evidence there is a great deal of discussion of problems of promotion, but little awareness of the overall need to evoke a dynamic of progress. Again, some of these issues were posed to the Commission. For example, the Executive and Higher Officers' Association had some useful points to make about the training of officials for their duties and the use of an adequate system of annual reporting to help people to give of their best.

One is conscious, therefore, of an honest, hardworking, loyal public service performing, and expected to perform, the straightforward, unimaginative role of carrying into effect ideas that were formulated elsewhere. This is clearly the major premise of the Commission Report. They are not wholly to be blamed for this. On it they got no lead whatever from the Department of Finance. Only the staff associations, particularly those representing the executive officers and the clerical officers, had a glimmering of the nature of the problems of a civil service in a country urgently needing economic and social development.

III

LOCAL GOVERNMENT

Secondly, local government.

In the local government sphere the tale is different. First, Sinn Féin had a policy about local government. The Poor Law unions were swept out of existence in 1923 and the rural districts in 1925. Thus, generally speaking, the county became from 1923 the unit of administration. In this way a decisive break was made with the multiplicity of small authorities that is one of the perennial problems of local government.

Secondly, and more fundamentally, there was grasped the nettle of what are the responsibilities of the central authority in relation to local government. It was clearly recognised that there would have to be central leadership and control if changes were to be made with any degree of effectiveness. Thirdly, to concentrate business into relatively large authorities is to raise the administrative problem in a big way. The volume of business – as was rapidly recognised, though not so rapidly acted upon – made it impossible for adequate administration to be carried out by public representatives in their spare time. It had to be professionalised.

For this reason three substantial steps were taken from 1925. The first of these was to establish a single local government service instead of a separate service for each local authority. This was done simply by linking up, for superannuation purposes, service between different local authorities. Secondly, in the following year, the Local Appointments Commission was established. This provided that, for anyone who was not already an officer of a local authority, appointment to a senior administrative or professional post in the service of any local authority would have to be filled after public advertisement and a competition conducted by the Local Appointments Commissioners in Dublin. Provision was also made that the Minister for Local Government and Public Health could apply this system of open advertisement and public competition conducted by the commissioners to other posts. This power was fairly extensively used. Most significantly, the problem of promotion was resolutely faced. The Act provided that an existing pensionable officer of a local authority could be promoted to one of the posts to which it applied if the appointment were made within three months and if the minister approved. Otherwise the post had to be publicly advertised and filled through the Commission. As a general rule the minister was not prepared to approve of promotion in this way. The net result was that the local government service had a recruitment and promotion policy for its most senior posts that ensured that, so far as humanly possible, only the best qualified people were recruited and received advancement. In these two matters, in the positive lead given by the Department of Local Government and Public Health and the use of the Local Appointments Commission as both a recruitment and promotion body, the local service tackled problems, admittedly pressing problems, that the civil service has not even yet got around to facing.

The next, and second most important stage in the professionalisation of the work of local government, was to establish the city and county management system, an idea borrowed and adapted from the United States. Separate commissions recommended this for Dublin in 1926, and for the counties in 1927. It was first applied, at local request, in Cork in 1929, and then spread to Dublin in 1930, to Limerick in 1934 and to Waterford in 1939. It was extended to the counties in 1940.

All these were positive steps to adapt the English system of local government to the needs of the community as perceived at that time. The momentum of these changes was later to be lost, but in the period we are considering they contrast strikingly with the laisser faire attitude adopted towards the civil service. The significant factor here was that, often in conditions of great controversy, the central body realised its duties of leadership and the need to adapt old institutions to new needs.

IV

STATE-SPONSORED BODIES

Thirdly, the state-sponsored bodies.

We have seen that in 1924 it was decided to tidy up, so far as possible, the number of boards and other public bodies that had grown up under the British administration and to concentrate them within the civil service under the control of ministers. In this way, because ministers were answerable to the Dáil, and civil servants had no power of action other than as part of the minister's extended personality, there would be complete public control over the administration. Thus, the Congested Districts Board, which had a representative board and independent sources of funds, not all of whose staff were civil servants, was firmly incorporated in the civil service.

Within three years the process of reversing all of this, and of much else besides, which is now flowing so strongly, was begun. This was to be expected. If there was to be development, and if the civil service was not to be regarded as a development agency, then new forms of institutions had to be invented. What was not realised was that to create new institutions without making changes in the way public institutions were to behave was at best to postpone the day when the reform of all the institutions would be necessary. The year 1927 saw the invention of the state-sponsored body which has now become so important a part of the administrative life of our community. In that year were created the Dairy Disposals Company, to take over surplus creameries; the Electricity Supply Board to generate and distribute electricity; the Agricultural Credit Corporation to make loans to farmers; the Currency Commission, the predecessor of the Central Bank; and the Medical Registration Council. In 1933 were created the Irish Sugar Company, the Industrial Credit Company and the Hospitals Commission; and in 1936, Aer Lingus. Other, smaller or experimental, bodies were set up in the intervening years. The main point here is that these bodies were set up on an ad hoc and functional basis, thus completely reversing the trend of the 19th century which had been to try to have a small number of generalised bodies, with a single civil service staff, recruited through a single agency, with single conditions of service and so on. In 1927 it was decided to abandon this principle in the interests of giving freedom of operation outside what were believed to be the stifling conditions of civil service life. As we have seen, it was taken for granted that the civil service itself was not to be a development agency.

Not all the state-sponsored bodies were designed to be development bodies (such as the Medical Registration Council) but a number were. Not all of these have been unqualified successes. For example, it took the Agricultural Credit Corporation more than 30 years of life before it began to play a genuinely developmental role in our community. Others have responded well to the natural dynamism of progress; the striking examples here have been the Electricity Supply Board and Aer Lingus. A small number have shown genuine creative and promotional abilities, against the current of the times. The most striking of these has been Bord na Mona, whose main activities fall outside our period, and the Irish Sugar Company whose period of most striking development did not take place for perhaps quarter of a century after its foundation. The point here is that the creation of new institutions did not of itself change the substantially passive climate of official thinking even when new bodies, free of what were believed to be the undue civil service constraints, were created.

The great achievement of the state-sponsored bodies has been, of course, to establish that Irish public bodies can run practical affairs as competently as anybody else, to give employment especially to professional men and technologists in the building up of their own country which would not otherwise be available to them, and to contribute effectively to the overall development of the community.

V

APPELLATE GOVERNMENT

Of the fourth branch of government, appellate government, there is not much to say. In general, a free society requires that the individual who has a grievance against a public body should have the right to a fair hearing and either redress or compensation. This problem had long been recognised on the Continent of Europe and the remarkable institution of the *Conseil d'État* in France and in a number of the other European countries was developed over the 19th century to provide a regular system by which the citizen in his disputes with the administration could gain satisfaction.

In 1930 the British Lord Chief Justice, Lord Hewart, in his book *The New Despotism* attacked two developments: the tendency of Parliament to transfer to ministers some of their legislative powers, and the tendency to transfer from the courts to ministers a number of judicial functions. The practice of giving to ministers the power of making statutory regulations has not been deflected by these, and other more temperate, criticisms; but in Britain there has been much discussion, which is now in the past few years bearing fruit, of the means of regularising the procedures for hearing quasi-judicial appeals. The same tendencies could be seen to operate in Ireland during the 1920's and 1930's and indeed since; but the need to devise anything other than ad hoc solutions for this kind of problem has never emerged into the public consciousness and little or nothing was done to tackle one of the basic problems of public administration.

VI

CONCLUSION

In conclusion, if one has to cast up a balance sheet of Irish public administration in the decade under review, one is left with a nagging doubt. On the assets side are those that have been inherited from our previous masters, a well organised and educated public service, strikingly loyal, honest and hard working. It did not spare itself in carrying out policies that were settled somewhere else. On the debit side is the great gaping hole represented by the failure to solve the deep rooted economic and social problems of the country. These are the tests by which the performance of governments nowadays is judged, and in modern societies the public service is expected to play a big part in helping Governments to solve these problems. One can divide the operation of government in action into two kinds – the formulating of new policies, and the implementing of those policies. So far as implementation is concerned the conventional virtues are probably adequate enough; but adequate implementation itself depends on the adequate formulation of new and relevant policies. Trevelyan, the great reformer of the British civil service in the middle of the 19th century, said his reform was based on 'the fundamental proposition that the business of government was to be carried on by those who think as to what ought to be done, and not by those who do what must be done.' It was this problem of posing the oughts for public action that was so completely neglected in the period under review. This itself arose from a remarkable intellectual neglect of the problems of government. Consider for example, the problem of the role of the state in a democratic community. In Ireland basically conflicting polices were carried on. The premises on which the industrial revival was based were quite opposed to those from which the financial management of our community was derived; this basic conflict was not adequately faced or resolved. Secondly, little attention was paid to the possible uses of new administrative techniques. Planning and programming, which have now been shown to have tremendous administrative utility, were words of abuse in the 1920's and 1930's; dispassionate consideration of these techniques might have helped to solve many problems in the 1920's and 1930's that had to await another generation. Less excusably, very little attention was paid to the problems of human dynamics within the public service. The public service had a remarkable natural advantage at that time in attracting to itself most of the intelligent young people in the country. When it recruited them, however, it did not seem to know what to do with them. The conventional virtues of honesty, hard work, devotion to duty – these were inculcated by precept and example. This was a very good thing to do, but the really valuable qualities of creativity and imagination were not as a matter of policy evoked from these talented young people.

When one looks back on the achievements and problems of the country in the 1920's and 1930's one sees, so far as public administration was concerned, a patchwork of much that was well done and much that was left to a later generation.

THE MINORITY PROBLEM IN THE 26 COUNTIES

F. S. L. Lyons

In talking to-night about the minority problem in the Irish Free State I shall take it that my main concern is with those, unionist in politics and mainly Protestant in religion, who found themselves in 1921 faced with an effort of read-justment far more drastic than they could have imagined five, or even three, years earlier. If I had to describe their reaction to this new situation in a single sentence, I should say that it was that of the dog in the night in the Sherlock Holmes story. The significance of that dog, you may re-member, was that it didn't bark. And, broadly speaking, one may say of the ex-unionist or loyalist minority that the most important thing about it is that it too hasn't barked since the Treaty.

Now this silence is, of course, open to two quite different interpretations. A minority may not bark because it is afraid to bark, or it may not bark because it has no cause to do so. Both these interpretations are in a measure true of the southern minority. Undoubtedly at the outset, and perhaps also for a short period after 1932, they were afraid to bark; equally, at other times they clearly had no reason to bark, and it is these fluctuations between moods of almost total alienation and periods of relative tranquil-lity which form the main thread in their history during the period covered by these lectures.

Before we can trace these fluctuations, however, we must be clear about the size and composition of the minor-ity. It had always been very small – even the most hope-ful estimates at the time of the Treaty place it at about 250,000 – and it tended to get steadily smaller during the period we are considering. Even if we equated it with the Protestant community *en bloc* (which would in fact be a gross over-simplification) it was still no more than 7 per cent of the total population in 1926, or 6 per cent in 1936.

Not all of these, of course, were ex-unionists and, if we are to think of the minority as ex-unionist, then its share of the total, even including a remnant of Castle Catholics who had backed the wrong horse, would probably be nearer to 5 or even 4 per cent. Even this tiny minority was quite sharply divided between those who would have nothing whatever to do with the new regime and the daring few – like Lord Midleton or the distiller, Andrew Jameson – who felt that the best hope for the future was loyal co-operation. This lack of cohesiveness was further emphasised by the fact that while the southern unionists were heavily concentrated in one or two areas – chiefly south county Dublin and parts of Cork – elsewhere they were pitifully thin on the ground.

Historically, these southern unionists had been closely identified with the landed gentry, who for generations had played a key part in local government and also had provided considerable employment, as well as setting the tone for rural society. These functions had begun to be eroded by the reforming legislation of the late nineteenth and early twentieth centuries. When local government became elective – and therefore nationalist – after 1898, and when five years later the Wyndham Act accelerated the sale of the large estates, it became obvious that the days of the great Anglo-Irish landlord caste were over. Some left the country after selling up, and many others departed either during the Anglo-Irish war, or because of the insecurity of life and property after the Treaty. A number, however, remained and it would be easy to name families in every part of the country which still live in their ancestral homes and which still play, on a more restricted scale, the kind of role their forbears took for granted. More restricted, partly because they are generally poorer than they used to be, but also because the confidence and poise of the class as a whole have been irretrievably broken.

But of course the minority was not, and never had been, solely based upon the land. Traditionally it had played a part in the commercial life of the country out of all proportion to its numbers and, although this naturally diminished somewhat after 1921, it remained very important. In the retail trade in Dublin, for example, especially among the general stores, the grocers and the hardware merchants, as builders' providers, as the owners of chains of cafes and restaurants, as hoteliers and caterers, in the management of banks and insurance companies, as well as in such larger enterprises as Jacob's, Jameson's, Guinness' and other breweries in various parts of the country, they continued to prosper and out of their prosperity to contribute to the economic benefit of the country as a whole. And beyond question, a major factor in reconciling the minority to the Irish Free State was its speedy realisation that Mr. Cosgrave's government was sympathetic to the business world in which they were so involved.

There was, however, quite another way in which the minority had for long played a very special role in Irish society and one of the most crucial questions after 1921 was how far it could go on playing that special role. In 1925, in an otherwise ill-conceived speech which he made in the Senate on the divorce legislation then pending, W.B. Yeats gave this interpretation of the historic significance of the minority:

'We are,' he said, 'no petty people. We are one of the great stocks of Europe. We are the people of Grattan; we are the people of Swift, the people of Emmet, the people of Parnell. We have created the most of the modern literature of this country. We have created the best of its political intelligence.'

This, you may say, was exaggeration – magnificent, but still exaggeration. Yet, in literature at least, there was some substance to the claim, especially if you add to his list the names of Synge and Lady Gregory and Yeats himself. How far did this impetus persist into the post-Treaty period, when the political and social conditions that had produced the fine flowering of Anglo-Irish culture had vanished? Merely to ask the question is to reveal how completely the minority had shrunk into itself after 1921. Some notable figures there were, indeed – the painter Jack Yeats, and Lennox Robinson in the theatre, while W.B. Yeats, if something less than adequate as Senator, nevertheless lived on to write some of his finest poetry in his native land. But these men were all survivals from an earlier age – little talent of any comparable vigour or freshness emerged from the post-Treaty generation, and it is ominously significant that the most arresting of the newer figures, Samuel Beckett, was a far more complete exile from his culture than Joyce ever had been from his. The fact is that the intellectual centre of gravity of the country had shifted and the rising names of the 'twenties and 'thirties were almost all those of young men from Dublin or Cork, or the remoter hinterland, who owed little to the past and whose university, as likely as not, had been the Civil War.

What I am saying, I suppose, is that in the arts generally, as in political and social life, the minority had fallen back onto the defensive. And this was equally true in other sectors of the intellectual and professional life of the country. In the learned professions, indeed, they were still strongly represented and in medicine especially they remained deeply entrenched, though even here it was noticeable that Trinity exported many of its best young doctors and that the hospital which Protestants all over the country regarded with particular affection as their own – the Adelaide – now first began to feel the pressures of economic stringency. Even more marked was the changing balance in the law. In the nineteenth century a legal career had been one of the most popular avenues to advancement for an ambitious young man – Carson and the first lord Glenavy are only two obvious examples – but even in the nineteenth century the Catholic and nationalist element at the bar had been increasing, and this tendency was naturally accentuated after 1921, to such a degree indeed that although successive governments strove always to have the minority represented on the bench, it was becoming steadily more difficult to find men of sufficient calibre. Anglo-Irish lawyers did continue to become judges, but too often in Malaya or Africa or the West Indies, and not frequently enough at home.

To speak of individual artists, or even of professional groups, does not of course give us a broad enough view of the minority as a whole. We have also to look at its most characteristic institutions. In former times the ascendancy had rested on a kind of quadrilateral made up of the Viceregal Lodge, Dublin Castle, the Church of Ireland and Trinity College. Since, after 1921, the first two of these had passed into other hands, the Church of Ireland and Trinity remained alone in unenviable isolation. For the Church of Ireland, it is true, the material change was not perhaps so very drastic, Gladstone having already clipped its wings fifty years earlier. Nevertheless, there was intense anxiety about the degree of tolerance which would be extended to religious minorities generally under the new regime, and it was fortunate indeed for Protestants that at this critical moment the Church of Ireland found in Dr. Gregg, Archbishop of Dublin, a leader who was able to face the new situation with courage, firmness and wisdom. He would himself have liked to see written guarantees of religious freedom for the minority and of protection for the corporate property of religious and university bodies, such as had been contained in the abortive Government of Ireland Act of 1920. Failing these, however, he was emphatic that the right course for his co-religionists to follow was loyally to accept the new constitution and to throw all their influence behind whatever forces were working for peace and order. This was how he put it in a public statement made in December 1921 after the terms of the Treaty had been published:

It concerns us all that we should have a strong capable and wise government. And therefore it concerns us all to offer to the Irish Free State so shortly to be constituted our loyalty and our good will. I believe there is a genuine disposition on the part of those from whom we have differed in political outlook to make room for us and to welcome our co-operation, and we should be wrong, politically and religiously, to reject their advances. The new constitution will claim our allegiance with the same solemn authority as the one that is now being constitutionally annulled.

This was the line which he consistently took as Archbishop

of Dublin throughout the period with which we are concerned and in it he was followed, it is fair to say, not only by the Church of Ireland, but by the Protestant community as a whole. There were, indeed, things which irked them – for example, the operation of the Ne Temere decree, or of the censorship – and they remained extremely sensitive to anything remotely resembling bigotry amongst Catholic churchmen or laymen, but as the years went by without any encroachment on their religious liberties, as the new rulers of the State, of whatever party, set themselves to demonstrate a genuine toleration, these fears receded and in the generation which has grown up since the Treaty they are seldom to be found. This toleration has been so general that there is, perhaps, a disposition to take it for granted without realising how remarkable a phenomenon it was. Given the historical background, things could have been very different and it is only proper to acknowledge here that the almost total absence of religious discrimination in the new state must stand out as one of the major achievements of a self-governing Ireland.

The position of Trinity was more difficult, and in a sense, more critical. Throughout its history it had been closely identified with the ascendancy, and even though that identification was by no means complete – as the names of such graduates as Tone, and Emmet and Davis show – still it was unquestionably a pillar of the old regime. In the generation before the Treaty, Trinity made practically every political mistake it could make and the crude and ignorant gibes of Mahaffy and others at the renaissance of Irish culture aroused a deep resentment for which the university is still paying. By a curious irony, a Royal Commission in 1920 recommended the payment of an annual government grant to Trinity at the very moment when political events were taking the college far out of reach of the beneficence of the British Treasury. The Government of Ireland Act that same year stipulated that £30,000 per annum should be paid to Trinity from the Irish Exchequer, but when it became clear that the act would never take effect in the south the then Provost, Dr. Bernard, made frantic efforts to persuade Lloyd George to ensure that some comparable concession be written into the Treaty. In this he failed utterly and the college was left high and dry, with its revenues depleted, its hopes of a government grant disappointed, and an alien and largely hostile world at its gates.

Not unnaturally, the Fellows of that time retreated into their closed little society and had apparently no ambition beyond the mere wish to survive. The consequence, of course, was that whereas the contribution of the National University to the new state was incalculable, that of Trinity was negligible (at least in the early days) and it became a commonplace to describe Trinity as 'anti-national'. No doubt individuals did find it hard to adjust and did hanker after old times, but the Board of the College was quite clear where the University's duty lay in the future. On 10 December 1921 it passed a resolution urging Trinity's parliamentary representatives to support the settlement whose terms had then been published. 'The true interests of Trinity College can only be furthered by Irish peace', they asserted, 'and in the building up of happier conditions in Ireland the Board of Trinity College believes that Trinity men should take an active and sympathetic part'.

Perhaps this was asking a little much in the immediate aftermath of the Anglo-Irish war and the succeeding civil strife. The Fellows of that time were in no condition to take up positive attitudes, whether pro or anti-national, and what looked from outside like indifference or hostility was in reality timidity and bewilderment. The world had changed overnight and too many Fellows were too set in their ways to change with it. The result was that though individual scholars of repute were still in evidence, the 'twenties and 'thirties rank among the darkest periods of the College's history – it was poor, the buildings became steadily more dilapidated and a great tradition of learning seemed destined for extinction.

To anyone who, like myself, knew the place then as an undergraduate and has known it since as a Fellow, the transformation in the last fifteen years is almost miraculous. In material terms this has of course been mainly due to the generosity of successive governments whose grants have enabled a massive programme of modernisation to be carried out. But even more it is due to a profound change of attitude within Trinity itself, a change made possible by the simple passage of time. A new generation has grown up since the Treaty which knows nothing of the doubts and reservations of its predecessors, a generation which feels responsible for Trinity as a truly Irish university and asks only to be allowed to demonstrate that this is so.

This inability to come to terms with a new environment was not peculiar to Trinity – it was something experienced by most members of the minority in some part or other of their lives. This is to be explained, I think, partly by the suddenness and completeness of their reversal of fortune, which left them adrift without any familiar bearings, but partly also by the murderous attacks made against members of the first Senate of the Irish Free State in 1922. Many of the victims of these attacks belonged to the ex-unionist minority and several of them had long records of distinguished service to Ireland. The shock to their confidence was profound and lasting and it certainly did much to reinforce their traditional tendency to live very much to themselves. This in itself was not new of course. The political and religious divisions of Irish life had for centuries been paralleled by a kind of social apartheid – nationalist and unionist, Protestant and Catholic, living in two quite different circles which occasionally intersected in such places as the Royal Dublin Society or the Royal Irish Academy, but never by any chance coincided completely.

Before 1914, this separateness was simply a part of their mystique as a governing caste and if it seemed to those outside the charmed circle to be an entirely unjustified arrogance, it was largely an unselfconscious arrogance. After 1921 the arrogance disappeared, but so did the unselfconsciousness. Now on the defensive, the minority became intensely aware of their isolation and withdrew into a kind of ghetto. A ghetto can be just as much a state of mind as a physical locality and if I, as one who grew up in this rather stifling atmosphere, had to say what seems to me the most striking characteristic of the minority in the twenties and thirties, it is the persistence of precisely this ghetto mentality. It expressed itself in all sorts of ways, some trivial, some more important. For example, it is a small but significant pointer that many ex-unionists continued to speak of Kingstown, not Dun Laoghaire, or that whenever the British team won the Aga Khan Cup at the Horse Show this was the signal for an almost hysterical rendering of God Save the King, which indeed, some at least of the minority never ceased to regard as *the* National Anthem. More important was the social isolation in which most of these people lived their lives, with the inevitable result of frequent inter-marriage, and social claustrophobia, so that to this day the first ten minutes of conversation between any minority group who don't know each other personally is likely to be devoted to finding out which of them is connected to which, by marriage or otherwise.

This in itself would not matter very much if it was not taken for granted — taken for granted by the majority too, one must add — that in all their social activities the minority would keep to themselves. Their parties, their sports, their clubs tended to be confined to 'their own sort' and it was all too rare for friendships to develop between them and the majority to the degree that visits would be exchanged between houses, or friends held in common.

But the most serious aspect of this segregation was the failure of the minority to make any significant impact on Irish politics. Their numbers, of course, were so few that even proportional representation, which they welcomed, could not make very much difference to them except in certain rather special areas, such as Donegal. Protestant membership of the Dáil was never large — in 1922 there were nine Protestants, in 1927 (the peak year) there were fourteen, but by 1938 that figure had been halved. And not all these Protestants were ex-unionists — indeed, one might fairly say that the only constant ex-unionist representation in the Dáil was the seats allotted to Trinity College and even these disappeared in the constitutional changes of 1936-37.

In the Senate, it is true, Arthur Griffith had promised

from the beginning that special provision should be made for representation of the minority and in the first Senate, especially, 16 out of the 30 Senators nominated by the government might reasonably have been described as ex-unionist, and this was quite apart from W. B. Yeats who, though certainly no unionist, was very conscious of his Anglo-Irish heritage. The sixteen included Andrew Jameson, Lord Glenavy, Sir John Keane, Sir Horace Plunkett, the Earl of Mayo, the Earl of Dunraven, Sir Nugent Everard, the dowager Countess of Desart and General Sir Bryan Mahon. Most of these had contributed greatly to Irish national development before 1914 and collectively they represented all that was best in moderate and enlightened unionism. Yet even when this is said, it is doubtful if this concession of special minority weight in the Senate was much more than a generous and reassuring gesture, for the good reason that the Senate itself was a junior partner in parliament. Consequently, although the minority spoke out on such matters as the final settlement of the land question, or the dangers inherent in the censorship legislation, and although Lord Glenavy and Senator J. G. Douglas in particular did much to uphold the Senate in its conflicts with the Dáil, one is left overwhelmingly with the impression that while what they had to say was important for the record, it did not have very much bearing on events.

The plain fact is that the minority could not really hope to exert much influence so long as it was consciously regarded as a minority. Integration, not segregation, was to be the only possible line of advance. And how to bring this about was the crucial problem they had to face, for, as Henry Harrison put it in 1924: 'Whether they would prefer to rest upon their special position, which sometimes gives rise to comment and criticism, or to emerge into the broader paths of normal citizenship, would be a matter for themselves'.

This, however, was not quite the whole truth. For many ex-unionists it did not seem to be entirely a matter for themselves. True, after the first shock of disillusionment, when it became clear that both the British government and their northern brethren were content to leave them to sink or swim by themselves, they did settle down under the Cosgrave government and many developed an allegiance to his party, which I suspect, though this can only be a personal opinion, was not shaken until Mr. Costello declared the Republic in 1948. The most remarkable instance of this was when Major Bryan Cooper, a former unionist M.P. and one of the outstanding exponents of conciliation, actually joined Mr. Cosgrave's party in 1927, but this was altogether exceptional.

With the advent of Mr. de Valera to power in 1932, however, this halcyon period came to an abrupt end. Their anxieties were immediately aroused and it is probable not only that a great many ex-unionists voted then for Mr. Cosgrave, but that a great many did so who had never voted at all since the inception of the State. The *Irish Times,* always in these years their spokesman, warned them repeatedly that it was their duty to vote for the Cosgrave government:

> There is the duty of self preservation. If Fianna Fáil takes office, the wealth and security of every citizen, including the ex-unionists, will be impaired and, perhaps, gravely imperilled. There is the duty of loyalty to Ireland and to the Empire. If Fianna Fáil takes office, the Free State's carefully fostered prosperity will wither, and she will became an Ishmael from that Empire which the ex-unionists, their sons and their ancestors, have helped to mould.

In the light of events these dire prophecies may seem grotesque, for the historian of the future may well establish that the main credit for the ultimate reconciliation of the minority, not just to the Irish Free State, but to the Republic, will belong precisely to Mr. de Valera and his party. On the short term, however, there certainly seemed some substance in the warnings of the *Irish Times*. The outbreak of the Anglo-Irish economic war, the whittling away of the outward and visible signs of dominion status, the revision of constituencies increasing the number having less than five members and therefore making it more difficult for minority interests to gain seats, the abolition of university representation in the Dáil, and above all the abolition of the Senate itself – these were successive shocks to the confidence of the ex-unionists and up to the end of the period with which we are here concerned their attitude to Fianna Fáil remained one of sullen resentment. In 1937 the task of reconciling them to the new regime was still far in the future – it has in fact been mainly the work of the past fifteen years – but it was a task of fundamental importance to the state, for they still had much to contribute to Ireland. They were, and were conscious of being, 'no petty people', whose allegiance was a prize worth any statesman's winning.

'EDUCATION IN THE NEW IRELAND'

Rev. Séan Ó Catháin, S.J.

As in other aspects of Irish life, the period from 1927 to 1939 was to be a time of testing for education too. The five years since the founding of the Irish Free State had seen great changes both in the organization and in the content of the country's schooling. On the other hand the new political situation brought about few changes in the Universities and so I exclude higher education from this discussion.

I shall first describe the changes that took place in the schools and examine how some of them worked out. And then I shall discuss some new developments in education in the period which concerns us.

In the organization of education the most important change was in administration. Before 1921 each of the various types of schools had its own separate administrative body. The primary schools, for example, were controlled by the Commissioners of National Education; the technical schools – in so far as they existed – were looked after by a Department of Agriculture and Technical Instruction. And so on. By 1924 these schools – there were five types in all – had been brought under a Minister of Education who presided over one Department with three main branches: primary, secondary and technical.

Under organization we may also mention a measure taken to improve the quality of candidates entering the Training Colleges for primary teachers. In 1926 four Preparatory Colleges were set up. These were residential schools owned by the Department of Education. Entry to them was by competitive examination, but with a heavy bias in favour of those who reached high marks in oral Irish, and the course was one of four years leading to the Leaving Certificate. Here we may note that the Department by-passed one of its own new regulations – that which stated that the minimum length of the course was to be five years. By the end of our period, the year 1939, there were six of these Colleges in existence and they supplied about one-third of the yearly intake into the Training Colleges.

The third point to be mentioned under organization is the School Attendance Act of 1927. An Attendance Act had indeed been passed as far back as 1892, but its operation had been left to the discretion of the local authorities. We are fond of talking about the 'traditional love of the Irish people for learning.' It may then be interesting to point out that in 1921 the average school attendance of children under fourteen years of age was only about 50%. The new Act laid down that children between the ages of six and fourteen must attend school unless validly excused. It also gave power to the Minister to extend the school-leaving age to sixteen.

Apart from these three changes, no other administrative change was introduced. Except for the Preparatory Colleges, there was no attempt at State ownership of the schools. The primary and secondary schools remained essentially what they had been: private institutions supported financially in varying degrees by public money and theoretically free to conduct their own affairs. How far they were in fact free is another matter. As for the small number of technical schools, they remained, as they had been, under the control of the local authority.

When we come to the content of the schooling it was a very different matter. The changes here were fundamental and far-reaching. It is no wonder that they gave rise to controversies at the time; controversies that have not yet died away. We may examine these changes under two headings: the examination system and the curriculum.

In the primary schools the change of government did not bring about any immediate change so far as examinations went. I say 'no immediate change' for, as we shall see, later on in our period an examination was introduced. In the secondary schools, however, a radical change was made. To show what the change was, I must say something about the earlier system.

Up to 1924 there were three examinations: Junior Grade, Middle Grade and Senior Grade. Each of these was a test of the work done in one year on very detailed courses of instruction. Because the unit of time was so short and because the courses were so cut and dried, this system could and did lead to a good deal of cramming. But there was a much more urgent reason for making success in these examinations a very vital matter. The chief financial aid which the schools got from the State was a grant based entirely on the number of successes they achieved in these examinations. It requires very little imagination to picture to oneself the overwhelming stress that was laid on success in them. The system explains, too, the words of the teacher quoted by Pearse: 'Culture is all very well, but if you don't stick to your programme your boys won't pass.'

The Act of 1924 put an end to this vicious 'Results System.' The State grant was now based on the number of pupils in the school who were following a course of studies approved by the Department. How they fared in any one examination did not affect this grant.

Instead of the yearly examinations, two were set up: the first – the Intermediate Certificate Examination – was to be a test of the work done over a period of three or four years and the second – the Leaving Certificate Examination – came at the end of a further two years. The lengthening of the time of preparation was intended to lighten the stress on both master and pupil, to give more elbow-room as it were for a leisurely and more fruitful form of learning.

This aim was intended to be further helped by a very big step – there were to be no more prescribed texts. I cannot do better here than quote from the first annual Report of the Department, that for the combined years 1924-26: 'Under the old system the programmes had been, with few exceptions, rigid and narrow, and had to be carried out through the study of prescribed texts on which the examinations were based. Under the new system the programmes are of the widest and most elastic types, prescribed texts have been abolished in all subjects, and the schools now enjoy the maximum of freedom both as regards the range of their programmes and the choice of books to suit their particular needs.'

We may as well finish the story of this change here as it began and ended almost within the period we are talking about. Set texts began to re-appear in 1939 and by 1941 they were prescribed in all language subjects. I have been told that this came about entirely at the request of the schools themselves. What made them go back to the old system? Two things did so, I believe. The first was a matter of tradition. Old ways of acting, and so of teaching die hard. Teaching methods which for over forty years had been based on set texts could hardly be changed overnight. Maybe some schools and teachers did not give the new plan too whole-hearted a sympathy from the beginning. It does seem now, looking back on it, that the scheme was too radical, that better results might have come from a more gradual abolition of the set texts. Secondly, you had the combination of this 'open' course with one external, uniform examination for the whole country. To set an examination on such widely diversified courses so that it could test what had been done without distorting it was apparently impossible. Whatever about the more intelligent pupils, the difficulties of preparing a pass class for those examinations will still, even at this lapse of time, be vivid in the memories of many teachers.

If the aim of the new system of examining was to give the schools more freedom, more independence in teaching, how far was that aim attained in the first fifteen years? Not very far, I'm afraid. Even with the best co-operation from the Department, it would have needed a real effort, as we have seen, for schools and teachers to shake off an attitude of mind towards the examinations which they had developed over the years. But the Department did something which, looking back at it today, we now see was a grievous mistake. Every year the results of the examinations with the marks which each pupil got in each of his subjects were published in book form. Only the examination number of the pupil was given, it is true, but the name of each school was printed at the head of its respective batch of numbers. The results of such a practice can be easily imagined. A deplorable spirit of rivalry grew up; schools advertised their annual successes as if they were purely commercial concerns, and the idea took firm root and was to develop in the coming years that the only test of a school's efficiency was how its pupils did in the examinations. The practice of publishing the name of the school was abandoned after some years, but the damage was done.

This is not the place to speak of the cramping and stultifying effects of an external, uniform examination on the education of a country. I have my own very strong views on that point. But this much I must say: the framers of the new secondary system in Ireland had a wonderful chance to make a new beginning and they missed it. It was not that they were without guidance. Even at that period a good deal had been written in English about the evils of the external examination. Even at that period they had the example of other countries which had rejected the system without chaos taking over. But there was no need to go outside their own country. They need not have looked further than Pearse. I wonder how many of them remembered his impassioned plea for freedom in our schools? Let me quote what he wrote just fifty years ago as he looked forward to education in a free Ireland: 'Well-trained and well-paid teachers, well-equipped and beautiful schools, and a fund at the disposal of each school to enable it to award prizes on its own tests based on its own programme – these would be among the characteristics of a new secondary system.' But in 1924 Pearse was dead, and his followers could do no better than to set up, with the best intentions in the world, one more form of external examination – a form which they found ready to hand in the proposals of a Vice-Regal Commission of 1919.

I turn now to the content of the new education – to the curriculum. And here, of course, the new factor that influenced most strongly both primary and secondary schools was the State policy to work for the restoration of Irish as the common language of the country, and in particular the decision to entrust to the schools a very large part in that work.

108

Let me summarize here the means that were adopted. First, in the primary schools: (1) the whole work of the Infant classes was to be done through Irish as soon as possible; (2) the use of Irish as a medium of instruction was to be introduced step by step into the classes of the primary school proper; (3) a number of proposals were made to ensure that there would be enough properly-qualified primary teachers for this work. In the secondary schools: (1) special stress was laid on the teaching of Irish, with the intention of soon making it an obligatory subject; (2) special inducements – in the form of extra grants and salary payments, and bonus marks at examinations – were offered to schools which used Irish, either wholly or partially, in the work of the school; (3) special awards were offered for fluency in speaking Irish, and (4) all secondary teachers had to pass an oral examination in the language before they came to be what was called 'recognized.'

Now it is obvious that I cannot hope to trace through our period the success or failure of all the measures the Government adopted. But there are three points that I should like to make. First of all, the policy of barring English from the Infant classes. This is the step which caused and still continues to cause the most bitter of controversies. There is no point in repeating here what has been said on either side, but I should like to put one fact before you. This particular proposal was adopted from the conclusions of both the first and second National Programme Conferences which were called to determine what the new curriculum in the primary schools would be. The primary teachers through their organization – the Irish National Teachers Organization – were represented on those conferences and gave their assent to the proposal, and during the years of our period they tried to put that proposal into practice. And then, in 1941, the INTO published the report of a Committee of Enquiry into the use of Irish as a teaching medium to children whose home language was English. Though the report is not above criticism in details, it is clear that there was a very wide opinion among the teachers that the results of the policy were in no way commensurable with the labour imposed on the teacher and the strain to which the children were alleged to be subjected. And that this applied in particular to the Infant classes. So far as I know, no answer was given to the points made, and note that the teachers were the only people – apart from the children, of course – who had first hand experience of what was happening; but the policy continues virtually unchanged.

Secondly, I want to draw attention to the fact that the chief point in the policy was to make the pupils fluent Irish speakers. This is, of course, obvious. It was a vernacular that was to be revived, not a language for reading or writing only. But here the teachers, in the secondary and to a less extent in the primary schools, came up against the crippling effects of the external examination.

In most secondary schools Irish quickly became just one more subject that had to be taught for the written examination, but a subject that very soon carried in the eyes of parents and children the negative value of being 'compulsory' when, in 1928, it became an essential subject on the school curriculum, and in 1934 success in it was made a condition of passing the Certificate examinations. There were the Inspectors of course who were supposed to test for fluency, but an occasional visit from an Inspector was of little avail against the ever-present pressure of the examination. In short the teaching methods used tended to prepare pupils principally for the written test and no more. During our period one reads in the annual Reports of the Department frequent criticisms of the quality of the oral work in the schools.

The pressure of the examination was to make itself felt in the primary schools too, for in 1929 what was called the Primary School Certificate Examination was started. This was a written test in three subjects – Irish, English and Arithmetic – which the pupil was to take at the end of the normal primary course. It was a test which, as time went on, was to create a good deal of opposition among teachers. They saw that success in it could often be bought only by neglecting the other subjects which were not examined, but what concerns us here is that the prospect of the written test in Irish tended to the loss of that fluency that

110

had been achieved in the lower classes. However, during our period the examination was not compulsory – in 1936, for example, only 10% of the children took it – so that its full effects were not yet felt.

To close this discussion on the question of Irish in the schools, I think it necessary to say something about the general policy. This seems to have been that if the schools succeeded in making the children fluent Irish speakers the greater part of the battle for Irish would have been won. In fact, as we know now, by and large the schools did not succeed. But let us suppose for a moment that they had done so, would Irish be well on the way to being the common language of the country? I believe that a fundamental mistake was made here. So far as I have read in the history of education, what goes on in the schools of a community, of a State is the end-result of what the people believe and wish and do. Schools never originate ideas, they follow them. That is to say, schools always lag behind the ideas and ideals of the adult community. Or, to put it in a way nearer to what we are thinking of here, I have never known or read of an example of schools that put through a social change that the community as a whole did not want. Instances to the contrary may be presenting themselves to some of you, but if you examine them carefully you will see that always a climate of opinion favourable to the change already existed outside the schools.

This is a most important point in this discussion, but for lack of time I can only put it before you in this way: the policy of restoring Irish by asking the schools to do the greater part of the work has failed so far simply because not enough people outside the schools could or would speak Irish. If you think that I am exaggerating let me quote from the Report of the Department for the year 1928–29.

'While it may be taken for granted that the revival of Irish cannot be effected without the co-operation of the schools, the question whether the schools' unaided efforts can accomplish this purpose is another matter, and is a question which it seems will shortly call for investigation. In many districts in which Irish is being well-taught in the schools, the language has little existence outside the school walls, and as far as the general use of Irish is concerned, little progress seems to have been made in the last ten years. It appears to be true that very few pupils speak Irish outside school hours, and a still smaller number can be still classified as Irish speakers a few years after leaving school. The Irish they have learnt is lost in the amount of English with which they have to deal on leaving school. English is the language of their sports and pastimes and of the means of earning their livelihood, while Irish remains a school subject closely allied to lessons and examinations. Under such circumstances it is inevitable that a very considerable part of the work done by the schools must fail to bear fruit, and failing help from outside, it may well be that the revival of the language may prove to be beyond their powers.'

So far, I have been talking to you about primary and secondary education. When we come to the technical schools we find, in the period we are considering, that a momentous step was taken. Under British rule, as a result of the Agricultural and Technical Instruction Act of 1899, a system of technical schools under the control of local authorities had been set up. The schools were financed partly out of local rates and partly by Government grants. In general we can say that they were confined to the towns and that most of the teaching was done in night classes. These schools, which were formerly run by a Department of Agriculture and Technical Instruction were now taken over by the Department of Education. For some years they continued to be run as they had been, until in 1930 the Vocational Education Act transformed both their organization and their curriculum. Indeed we could say that by the Act of 1930 the Department of Education raised the level of general education for many children who might otherwise have finished their schooling with the primary school, and provided opportunities for a higher degree of technical efficiency so vital in the economic life of the new State.

The schools were controlled by local committees which were elected by the local authorities. But once elected, the committees, under the Department of course, were in full control of the schools. This local control of the schools and the sense of personal responsibility it produced probably accounts for the satisfactory condition of the buildings and of the teaching given in them. But the Government too, whose own child, if I may put it in that way, these schools are has shown itself very generous both in the building and in the outfitting of them. In this respect, indeed, they are occasionally a source of jealousy to other schools, to the secondary schools in particular.

The new thing that these schools brought about was what is called Continuation Education. We take this form of education for granted nowadays, but it is well to remind ourselves what an improvement it brought about in the prospects of boys and girls who left schools at the primary level. Not only did it raise, as I have said, the level of their general education, with all the advantages that implies, but it gave them also some general practical training in preparation for taking up a trade later on. How successful the scheme has been is borne out, at least in the cities, by the annual rush for places in these classes each September.

I should also mention the new apprenticeship training in these schools. Up to 1930 it may be said that in any real sense of the word such training did not exist. With the Act, however, and especially since 1935 when a new scheme of trades examinations was set up by the Department, there has been a steady expansion of systematic training in these schools. This was to play a very important part in the economic growth of the country.

In this account of Irish education from 1924 to 1939 I have had to be selective in my choice of topics for discussion. Looking back on what I have said, I see that I have not sufficiently stressed the work done by a young and inexperienced government. I see for example that I have not mentioned what was done to tackle the enormous task of repairing and rebuilding the primary schools that had been handed over in a very neglected state. Nor on the other hand have I mentioned the increase in the number of secondary schools: from 278 in 1925 to 342 in 1939. This increase is all the more worthy of note when we remember that these 64 schools had to be built and equipped at private expense, that secondary education in this country is far from free, that what was called the Economic War with England came in the middle of our period, and that still parents were willing to make big sacrifices to give their children a good education. Perhaps I was wrong when, earlier on in this talk, I questioned the 'traditional love of the Irish for learning.'

THE LITERATURE OF THE PERIOD

Francis MacManus

In the ten or fifteen years after the establishment of the Irish Free State, the unhealed wounds of the civil war seemed beyond even the slow medicine of time. Time was at work, however. The conflict of black and white idealisms, the inhuman war of the angels, was becoming blurred by the everyday necessary business of living, by rebuilding, restoring farms, starting creameries and factories and making money. How did it all look to a receptive perspicacious mind at the beginning of the decade 1925 or 26 to 1936 or '37.

A mind of that sort was observing. It was AE's. We know what a fine blend he was of the practical and the visionary, of rural co-operativism and mystical poetics. In the summer of 1925 he was in Donegal and from there he wrote to the American writer and critic, Van Wyck Brooks, who spoke the same language of nationalism and always hoped that the spiritual would condition and rule the material in America as it appeared to have done in Ireland. AE wrote in prophetic mood:

> 'We in Ireland are reacting against the idealism which led us to war and civil war and I fear we are in for an era of materialism. Our new government is however honest and energetic and from a romantic conception of Ireland is being evolved the idea of a highly efficient modern state. I would like to live for fifteen years more because I think we will react again to the imaginative and spiritual and we shall probably begin a fight for spiritual freedom.'

So spoke the prophet who was, as we can tell after the events, both right and wrong. He was wrong in his expectation of a spiritual fight fifteen years or more hence.

True enough, there were fights for intellectual liberty against censorship; and for an Irish mind against the disappearance of the Irish language; and for more autonomy in Irish economics against British control. Yet, all those reactions weren't part of any general 'fight for spiritual freedom'. But AE was right in denoting that there was reaction against the idealism that had led to war and civil war.

Denis Johnston's play, that dramatised delirium of Irish history, *The Old Lady Says No,* belongs to the new mood. What he was saying was that patriotism isn't enough and he said it with all the weirdness and baroque elaboration of a dream. Two years later, in 1931, he was even more explicit in his more straightforward play, *The Moon in the Yellow River.* The young Irish government had initiated the Shannon hydroelectric scheme, a gigantic undertaking for an impoverished country. Here, in this play, the significance of such an effort was analysed and most vigorously expressed in language that echoed current history. The German engineer, Tausch, declares:

'*As Schiller tells us, Freedom cannot exist save when united with Might. And what Might can equal electrical power at one farthing a unit?... Soon you will be a happy nation of free men − free not by the magic of empty formulae or by the coats you wear, but by the inspiration of Power − Power − Power*'.

Against such idealised materialism − the Americans would preach it as world gospel after the Second World War − against such a doctrine the idealist Blake stood out in defiance.

'*Blake: The rest of the world may be crazy, but there's one corner of it yet, thank God, where you and your ludicrous machinery haven't turned us all into a race of pimps and beggars.*
Tausch: Machinery, my dear sir, does not make pimps and beggars.
Blake: It makes Proletarians. Is that any better?'

116

The dialectic may seem a bit forced for the sake of the drama but Mr. Denis Johnston did express part of the debate of the time. Something of the tension of the civil war crackled through the arguments. Blake represented the old political idealism, the poetic vision of the peasantry in conflict with the world of mechanized economic man.

In the same year as Mr. Johnston's play was produced, a book appeared which also went to the heart of the conflict. It was and is a major work of criticism and I know that my old friend, AE's correspondent, Van Wyck Brooks, confessed to having been profoundly influenced by it. The book was Daniel Corkery's, *Synge and Anglo-Irish Literature*. The book was, especially in its opening chapter, a challenge to Anglo-Irish literature to prove its credentials as Irish literature. It was, therefore, a political act as well as an exercise in literary criticism. And it came from a man who had been a mentor, a guide and philosopher of Irish nationalism, as well as the literary exemplar, for certain young Irish writers.

His book was an effort to make writers and critics take sides, commit themselves to profound views of the nation and its history. It was a continuation of the war for independence and, indeed, an extension of civil war. For his view was exclusivist, anti-colonial, fundamentally Gaelic and historically Catholic. He asked, 'what are we to say of Anglo-Irish as descriptive of that literature which had no existence until towards the end of the eighteenth century?' He did not see it as a literature written primarily for the nation, collaborated in by the people and warranted by the nation's own critical opinion. He saw it, in tendency, as a prey to English fashion. For him a normal literature was a national literature. But this literature wasn't normal. 'It is dependent' he wrote, 'on expatriates'.

Expatriates! The word roused voluble anger and years of resentment. To many writers of the time, it appeared to have offensive emotional associations, a suggestion of treachery or abandonment, as if expatriation were a different sort of emigration to that practised by farmers' sons' tradesmen, crafsmen and even priests. 'Expatriation' insisted Professor Corkery, 'is the badge of all the tribe of

Anglo-Irish literary men; and in nearly all cases it is a life sentence'. He named many of 'those wild geese' of the pen and asked where were they. Well, many of them are still alive, some back in Ireland. Some of them commuted between Ireland, Britain, the Continent and America. Most of them would have answered, as hundreds of thousands of other citizens could have answered decade after decade: we wanted for bread. Economics also affect letters.

Corkery, then, provided a canon for criticism but he did this less in his polemical first chapter of *Synge and Anglo-Irish Literature* than in the body of the work. He did grasp at one of the deep, almost subterranean problems of Irish history – the relationship between the native tradition and people, and the results of invasion. In the logic of his argument, however, there should be no writing in English in Ireland which includes his own magnificently written criticism and fiction. But he provided an escape hole. Padraic Colum and T.C. Murray, were 'excepted from this general condemnation'. They came from the people and wrote for them – an argument which, with a little honest manipulation can be applied to other writers. And applied it was in the course of the arguments that followed publication of *Synge and Anglo-Irish Literature*. But even as Professor Corkery wrote his landmark of a book, two of his disciples were emerging as first-ranking writers to join all the other writers who, expatriates or not, mostly wrote with the integrity of artists reacting to their world and time.

The two disciples were Frank O'Connor and Sean O'Faolain. Both had taken part in the Anglo-Irish war. Both had been idealistic patriots and Gaelic enthusiasts. Both were from Cork and both had learned from Corkery something of his immense respect and admiration for the short stories and novels of the Russians. Each made his debut with a volume of short stories.

Before going on to discuss them I should like to say, if indeed it's necessary, that this lecture isn't a comprehensive survey of the literature of the late 'twenties and the 'thirties. It is intended to be no more than a qualified glance, an attempt to suggest how some writers reacted to the new

Ireland. For this reason, there will be little or no reference to a great volume of worthy literature which poets, novelists and dramatists were creating – Padraic Colum, Mary Colum, Fred Higgins, Francis Stuart, Kate O'Brien, Lennox Robinson, younger men like Patrick Kavanagh and Robert Farren, to mention only a few. These were all writing free of any commitment to a particular political vision of the nation or to a sociological view of literature. Among many of them one could find suspicion of the State just as one could find in the State, as expressed through civil servants, a suspicion of them as queer fellows. In fact, the most consistent and permanent contact between the Irish State and Irish writers was through a state organ, the censorship board, which could ban with a savagery that seemed pathological. Because of the banning as well as the attrition of time, it was then difficult as it is now almost impossible to assemble here in full the necessary important novels and volumes of short stories for a study of the period. And it's safe to prophesy that, good as it was in quality, this literature will have a second strong effect on the Irish consciousness sometime in the future when it comes to be republished. It will be seen, for instance, that the beautifully written but banned novels by the poet Austin Clarke, *The Bright Temptation* (1932) and *The Singing Men of Cashel (1936)* were not so much vivid historical novels about medieval Ireland as satirical protests against the complacent morality of the Ireland of his own time.

Perhaps this was the sort of fight for spiritual freedom that AE had in mind. There is a story that during an immense religious celebration in Dublin during the early 'thirties, he was holidaying beside the sea in Donegal: and when a thunderstorm broke out in the sky in the direction of the capital, he stood half-naked on the rocks, shaking his fists and shouting out of his beard, 'Give it to them, give it to them'. It is a matter of history that his prayer wasn't heard. 'Them' were most of the people and in the mind of another novelist of the time, Francis Hackett, they, the people, had been deluded by clericalism. His solitary novel, *The Green Lion,* set in his native city and county of Kilkenny is a most sensuous and true evocation of place and people but altogether a *roman a these,* a story whose message twists the story. He saw, or at least one character in the novel saw, the Jesuits (and other religious orders) as a sort of universality that 'was a greater fraud than the fraud of the British Empire'. He went on:

'It was an encumbrance more alien to Ireland than Britain, and more destructive because the black alien was recruited from the native just like the Royal Irish police. Police or priest, they were governed by motives and moved by desires other than those which could give Ireland its healthy development. Remove this vast and greedy encumbrance, the intellect of Ireland would ripen and its heart be like the young lion's'.

This sort of romantic anticlericalism – some of the Fenians had it, too – was a product of frustrated nationalism of a fanatic heart robbed of its desires; it was far removed from the critical temper of Francis Stuart's sensitive and deeply religious novels, now out of print like so many books of the time; or from the savage satire of Liam O'Flaherty's *The Puritan,* which struck at 'piosities' with the fury of a warrior in a *riastradh;* or again, from the warm-hearted, compassionate social anger of Peadar O'Donnell's *Islanders* or *Adrigoole* – haunting pictures of rural life among the small farmers, the marginal men.

To return then to Professor Corkery's disciples: in 1931 Frank O'Connor's *Guests of the Nation* was published. Thirty years later, in the first wonderful volume of his autobiography, *An Only Child,* he described, with some irony, the childhood and youth, the experiences, the ardent commitments, the spiritual matrix out of which the short stories had come. He gave, as it were, a warranty of his own realism. His probing finger had, indeed, touched on the aching nerve. And the truth he uttered wasn't the sort of truth that a people accustomed to the commitments and cliches of patriotism, were expecting or even ready to expect. He was something new – excepting a few stories by Corkery – in all the literature about Irish war and he was new in that his vision clung to the humanity of the people about whom the stories were told. The title story, *Guests of the Nation,* is a classic about the pity, compassion and comradeship between men forced by the dictates of warfare to kill enemies who had become their friends. In the end, there were no enemies. There were just people, men, locked in a tragedy that had begun before they were born. But this tragic view is not O'Connor's only view. In the stories, *Attack, September Dawn,* and especially *Machine-Gun Corps in Action*, there is comedy. O'Connor had been committed and he had not only survived it but had come to laugh with much of the gaiety that had filled some of the fighters, Collins, for instance. Here then, in this first volume of stories, was the feel of a whole war, guerillas moving across a countryside in the shelter of ditches and hedges, running into and out of danger – but not as heroes for annual commemoration ceremonies and orations – just as men. The prose is loan, the narrative has a colloquial fluency and rhythm. It set the pattern of all his later writing, as in *Bones of Contention* which came five years later. The effect is quite different to that of Sean O'Faolain's more elaborate writing. O'Connor seems to strive, in perfection, towards the simplicity of the folktale; O'Faolain towards the more complex and lyrical apperceptions of the short story by Turgeniev or Chekov.

Mr. O'Faolain's disengagement from the world to which he had romantically and youthfully committed himself was for the sake of the deepening vision of life that informs his early short stories and novels. He, too, had mingled with the fighting men. To judge by the mood of his short stories, he had been, if anything, more romantic, more literary, more consciously the observant ironic writer, than had been Frank O'Connor. His first book, the collection of short stories, the banned *Midsummer Night Madness,* – there's a hint of romantic anthropology in the title – was published in 1932. It was the first of the four or five books, including one masterpiece of a novel, *Bird Alone,* that he would publish in the 'thirties'. The title story is about an old landlord and a young tinkerish sort of girl who are forced to marry by the local bullying republican leader, a bit of a blackguard, not at all a plaster hero. The story is all velvety night and fluttering birds and hoarse passion and violence and Irish rain. It may be a little far-fetched but it's effective more of disillusioned romantic than of the exasperated realist. And as for the compassion, that would be one of Mr. O'Faolain's chief and triumphant qualities in his later books. It is a dominant quality in his *A Nest of Simple Folk,* published in 1933, a massive novel in human terms about the humus, the roots, of Irish patriotism as manifested by the Fenians, the Parnellites and the men of the Easter Rising. Only Irish readers can appreciate the full significance of this book. This is the kind of historical burrowing which O'Connor never attempted. O'Connor would take as fact the struggle between the loyal R.I.C. man and his Sinn Fein son and tell a story around some one revealing incident, some event, in which the two revealed their humanity as a contrast to the antagonism of their profession of faith. In a way, O'Faolain was the more sophisticated writer, or rather, the writer who seemed to use more sophisticated methods of attaining the perfection of narrative that O'Connor, after the labour of a most careful artist, reached with apparent ease and simplicity. Moreover, O'Faolain was later more ostensibly in revolt.

As Dr. Conor Cruise O'Brien pointed out in his very perceptive essay in *Maria Cross,* there was in O'Faolain's writing 'a firm connection between the separate ideas of national, spiritual and sexual emancipation' – a complex which Dr. O'Brien calls 'parnellism'. But this was only one aspect of O'Faolain's maturing antagonism towards what he regarded as the provincialism of Ireland, its petty materialism mixed with crass romanticism, its gradual elevation of those top people who were no more than stuffed shirts, and in general, the poor quality of life. Naturally, he aroused antagonisms. In his journalism, rather than in his artistically conscientious novels and short stories, he reached for a pulpit or a soap-box and in the 'forties' became the editor of one of the most influential of Irish magazines, *The Bell.* Dr. Cruise O'Brien summed up his predicament in a series of sentences: 'It is exceedingly difficult to be a Catholic writer in a Catholic country: the pressure of a community varies inversely with its size; ingrowing nationalism destroys a writer's scope. Mr. O'Faolain has been a living example of the truth and interrelation of these three propositions'. He found being a writer difficult; the pressure of the small community to make him conform, was intense; and he did not allow his nationalism to narrow his scope. Indeed, he preached an international-ism that sometimes seemed like a reaction from confine-ment in the four green fields of Ireland.

For some of their readers, for one man in particular, both Frank O'Connor and Sean O'Faolain became the next-in-succession for the chieftainship of Irish letters. That one man was W.B. Yeats, Ireland's most eminent writer and, as T.S. Eliot was to say, the greatest poet of his time writing in English. One evening he did something that, for many observers, seemed rather odd. As a ban-quet in a Dublin hotel, he publicly bestowed his benedic-tion on the two Cork writers, bequeathing them his mantle, and – I quote Joseph Hone's biography – 'stating to the stupefaction of his listeners' that 'the future of Irish literature was with the realistic novel'. The cause of the stupefaction was that Yeats appeared to be handing over the glorious laurels of the poet for the not quite so noble overcoat that realistic novelists wear. Yet, the ageing poet must have genuinely believed that the realistic novel, or at least what he thought was the realistic novel, would in future dominate Irish literature. After all, Joyce's *Ulysses* was then fast being recognised as the novel of the age.

To declare that the future will go in a certain way, is one thing – however; the other is, that it didn't. Yeats still remained the High King. All during the years, almost to his death in 1939, this most political of genuine poets never ceased to take an interest in the course of Irish af-fairs. He had been a most effective and intelligent senator. He had had a decisive influence on the design of the new Irish coinage. He hungered for unity in Irish political life and he never ceased to regard politics with the proud eye of the aristocrat, the authoritarian, who linked Parnell with Burke and Swift. The nationalist milk which he had drunk when young still ran in his veins and he would salute the Easter Rising once more but with the perturbed heart of the prophet:

> *Some had no thought of victory*
> *But had gone out to die*
> *That Ireland's mind be greater,*
> *Her heart mount up on high;*
> *And yet who knows what's yet to come?*
> *For Patrick Pearse had said*
> *That in every generation*
> *Must Ireland's blood be shed.*

No man knew what was yet to come, though Yeats did feel that the world moved towards cataclysm. Like AE, indeed like many other Irish writers, he also felt that Ireland had more to give before she was engulfed by 'the filthy modern tide'. 'All those renowned generations' that defended Ireland's soul had to be justified; the alternative was too terrible to think about.

> *Fail, and that history turns into rubbish,*
> *All that great past to a trouble of fools.*

His great last poems were yet to come. They would be filled with memories of his old idols and friends, and admired acquaintances. Anger would stir in them, a heroic old man's anger looking on the world with a wry but lively hope. He would call on Casement's ghost, beating on the door of doom for an empire. Men reared on his earliest verse would find his new poetry rather strange, too strong, sometimes enigmatic as a nursery rhyme and violent with old rages. But the young would take to it. Before that last volume appeared, however, long before his last illness, he had a curious adventure.

He had always professed the aristocratic ideal and had been unashamedly on the side of the better part of the Ascendancy. Moreover, it is probably true that by autocratic character he was incapable of being democratic in the modern sense, thinking that democracy meant a form of faction fighting. So, he wrote:

> *When nations are empty up there at the top,*
> *When order has weakened or faction is strong,*
> *Time for us all to pick out a good tune,*
> *Take to the roads and go marching along.*

The political tune, so to speak, that he picked out was the rising motif of Fascism that was then setting two peoples of Europe on a long fateful march in black shirts and brown shirts. A fascist movement began in Ireland – a movement that was a reaction away from a state of affairs rather than an effort towards the realisation of a set of authoritarian political and social ideas. Very early in it's history, Yeats, became interested in the Blueshirt organisation. He invited the Blueshirt leader, General Eoin O'Duffy, out to his house at Riversdale, Rathfarnham, and as Hone says 'expatiated on Hegel and Spengler', which cannot have been of much help to a practical and somewhat unphilosophical man, such as O'Duffy was. How much did Yeats dramatise himself in this meeting? His letters are full of the excitement of the time, an excitement which, in different parts of the country, issued in ugly violence and bitter feelings. 'The interlocutors', says the biographer ironically, 'were somewhat at cross-purposes, but the General left with a promise of a song for his men'. In fact there was more than one song, written to the air of O'Donnell Abu:

> *Those fanatics all that we do would undo;*
> *Down the fanatic; down the clown;*
> *Down, down, hammer them down,*
> *Down to the tune of O'Donnell Abu.*

The songs weren't sung very much. It must not be forgotten that Yeats was tone-deaf. He had been led by his fanatic heart as he had been so often led in his long noble career, and now, once more, it led him to a disappointment. Again I quote his biographer, Hone: 'He was disappointed and was also surprised – it is a proof of the credulity which was often observed in him – when politics went on very much as before, the Blueshirts as demagogic as the rest'. In that credulity which was an aspect of innocence, and in that power of strong feeling as well as of coolly critical intelligence, he was all Irish:

125

Out of Ireland have we come;
Great hatred, little room,
Maimed us at the start.
I carry from my mother's womb
A fanatic heart.

He was not the only writer of those, not undistinguished years of the late twenties and early thirties to carry into Irish literature the qualities that history, geography, religion and blood had formed during 'that great past' which sometimes looked like becoming 'a trouble of fools'. There was no expatriation of the heart. Ireland was fastened to these writers like the flesh to the bone.

IRELAND: EXTERNAL RELATIONS
1926–1939

Nicholas Mansergh

There was one dominant factor in Ireland's external relations in the period 1926 – 1939. It was her membership of the British Commonwealth of Nations. In 1921 the Irish Free State became a Dominion. She was not, for reasons I suggested in a talk I gave on *The Dominion Settlement* in an earlier Thomas Davis series[1], a natural dominion. She had not, like Canada or Australia, moved gradually from colonial to dominion status; on the contrary, she had acquired a dominion status her leaders had never sought as a result, not of evolutionary, constitutional processes, but of revolutionary action. Nonetheless having become a dominion, the meaning, development, expansion and finally the supercession of that status became the chief preoccupation of successive Irish governments in their external policies.

Broadly speaking there were two possible Commonwealth policies for Irish governments after 1921. The first was to refashion the Commonwealth in closer accord with Irish interests and outlook; the second to seek the first opportunity to unravel, or by one dramatic revolutionary stroke to sever, Irish ties with the Commonwealth. These alternatives, again speaking very broadly, were pursued in turn by President Cosgrave's government from 1922 to 1932, and by President de Valera's administration from 1932 onwards. Behind them lay different assessments of Commonwealth potentialities, of Irish interests, not least in terms of national unity, and perhaps most of all of personal temperament and political instinct.

In 1926 the time was favourable for the pursuit of the first policy – that is to say, of a policy of constructive reinterpretation of Commonwealth ties in terms more

[1] Reprinted in Desmond Williams (ed.) *The Irish Struggle, 1916–1926* (London 1966).

congenial to Irish ears and more in accord with Irish interests and aspirations. In the summer of that year dominion leaders gathered together in London for an Imperial Conference. The emotions and thoughts of the day were summed up in one word – status. The principal task of the conference was to consider and, if possible, to define the status of the dominions and their relations with Britain. This may sound now an exercise in political abstractions; at the time, however, it was thought of, and probably rightly, as a last chance to reconcile dominion liberties with Commonwealth unity. Before he left Cape Town the South African Prime Minister, General Hertzog warned that he would set the veldt on fire with a campaign for republican independence if dominion equality with Britain were not recognized. The Conference, when it met, set up an Inter-Imperial Relations Committee to find a satisfying formula. Kevin O'Higgins was the Irish representative. He worked closely with the Canadians throughout and with the South Africans in the later stages. He felt that the direction was right, that substantial headway was being made and remarked that one would need to have been at the Imperial Conference of 1923 'to realize the vast change in our position'.[1] The chairman of this Committee was Lord Balfour, now in his old age and with memories of Mitchelstown far behind him. In Kevin O'Higgins's memorable comment, Balfour presided over the Committee's deliberations with 'a smile like moonlight on a tombstone'. But more important he produced a formula in a situation where a formula was not easy to find. The formula has passed down to history. It defined the relations of Great Britain and the dominions in these words: 'They are autonomous Communities within the British Empire, equal in status, in no way subordinate one to another in any aspect of their domestic or external affairs, though united by a common allegiance to the Crown, and freely associated as members of the British Commonwealth of Nations'.

To the Balfour formula all subscribed. But there were

[1] Quoted in T. de V. White, *Kevin O'Higgins*, London 1948, p. 221. See chap. XIV generally.

things contained in it which some delegates liked a good deal better than others – the Australians and New Zealanders, for example, being insistent on the opening references to the British Empire, the Canadians, South Africans and Irish placing all their emphasis on the concluding 'British Commonwealth of Nations'. There was no doubt, however, on which side the future lay. Equality was proclaimed to be the root principle of British Commonwealth relations. Equality meant, *negatively* the ending of legal or constitutional inequalities as between Britain and the dominions and *positively* the opening of the high road to further advances in dominion nationalism. The Commonwealth was well on the way to becoming, in fact as well as in name, a Commonwealth of Nations. That was important for all of them but more important for the Irish Free State than for any of them. 'We have brought home the bacon' said the South African Prime Minister, General Hertzog, to the cheering burghers of Pretoria. 'Irish bacon', commented Kevin O'Higgins tersely.

The equality proclaimed in 1926 was given practical application in succeeding years. At the Imperial Conference of 1930 and in the drafting of the Statute of Westminster, the Irish played their full part. Mr. Patrick McGilligan, the Irish delegate to the 1930 Conference, declared in July 1931 that, with the passage of the Statute of Westminster, the imperial system 'which it took centuries to build' was finally demolished. In its place there was a Commonwealth of Nations. It was not an Empire. It was an association of free and equal nations. And the Irish Free State was one among them. But was *it* free? Mr. McGilligan's political opponents were by no means convinced. What of the Treaty, that Treaty imposed under threat 'of immediate and terrible war?' What about the hated Oath of Allegiance? What about the Governor-General residing in the old Vice-Regal Lodge and symbolizing the presence of the Crown in the Constitution? What about Irish neutrality with the Treaty Ports in British hands? What about the right of secession itself? All these questions were asked; they were the coin of contemporary political controversy. And some at least of them were soon to be put to the test.

The second wave of Irish revolutionary nationalism sweeping Mr. de Valera into office early in 1932 ensured that – and a good deal more besides. The period of Irish refashioning of the Commonwealth ended before it had really begun.

To understand what followed in the second phase of Irish policy it is necessary to pause and reconsider some things from the past. The first article of the Treaty had declared that the Irish Free State should have the same constitutional status as the Dominion of Canada, the Commonwealth of Australia, the Dominion of New Zealand and the Union of South Africa, and the third Article more particularly defined Irish status by reference to that of Canada, the oldest dominion. The Treaty as a whole was vested with the force of fundamental law, both the Constituent Act and the Constitution declaring that if any provision of the Constitution, or of any amendment thereof, or any law made thereunder was in any respect repugnant to any provision of the Treaty, it was to the extent of such repugnancy 'absolutely void and inoperative.' But was there not and had there not been always the possibility of conflict here? Canadian status was not fixed; it was changing, it was developing fast. In Ottawa there was the Liberal Mackenzie King with his life-long suspicions of imperialist machinations in Downing Street to see to that! Was it not the case that under the earlier provisions of the Treaty, Irish status should likewise develop and advance? But what if such advances were in conflict with other provisions of the Treaty? Was Irish status then to be regarded to that extent as frozen and immutable? English diehard opinion took this view and sought to except the Irish Free State from the Statute of Westminster on that ground. President Cosgrave objected; the Irish Free State was not excepted. President de Valera came to office. He announced his intention of removing the Oath of Allegiance from the Constitution. It was mandatory under the Treaty – though President de Valera voiced his doubts even about that. But was it mandatory under the Statute of Westminster? President de Valera, it is true, did not pose this question; after all the Statute was a British enactment. He deployed instead arguments grounded in national right. He told J.H. Thomas, the Secretary of State for the Dominions on 22nd March, 1932, that the Constitution was the people's Constitution; that the government had an absolute right to modify it as the people desired. The people had declared their will. There was no ambiguity about their resolve to remove the Oath. It was a relic of medievalism and an intolerable burden. It was the cause of all the dissension in Ireland since the Treaty. It made friendly relations with Britain impossible. It was a test unparalleled in treaty relationships between states, and it had been imposed under threat of immediate and terrible war.[1] It had to go and it was clear it was going, whatever the British Government or the lawyers might say.

Was president de Valera in his assault upon the Oath challenging the sanctity of the Treaty settlement as a whole? Mr. Thomas, after some increasingly acrimonious exchanges, in which the area in dispute was widened both constitutionally and also economically by the Irish government's decision to retain Irish land annuity payments, was convinced that this was so. He maintained that the Oath was mandatory under the Treaty, that it was an integral part of the 1921 settlement and that the Treaty as a whole was an agreement 'which can only be altered by consent.' In brief, he took his stand upon the twin foundations of constitutional law and contractual obligation. President de Valera, on the other hand, as was evidenced by his rejoinder to J.H. Thomas of 5 April, 1932, continued to rest his case in the last resort upon indefeasible national sovereignty. 'Whether the Oath was,' he said, 'or was not an integral part of the Treaty made ten years ago is not now the issue. The real issue is that the Oath is an intolerable burden to the people of this State and they have declared in the most formal manner that they desire its instant removal'. They desired the removal of other things besides; and following the abolition of the Oath in 1933, there

---

[1] The statement of 22 March 1932, here summarized and the subsequent exchanges referred to below were reprinted in a British White Paper, Cmd 4056 and an Irish White Paper P. No. 650.

came a series of constitutional amendments culminating in the abolition of the office of the Governor-General, the keystone as it were of the dominion constitutional arch, in 1936. The Constitution of 1922 in consequence became a thing of shreds and patches and whatever validity the Treaty continued to possess, in contractual terms, it had lost in law since the Removal of the Oath Act 1933 deleted the 'repugnancy clause' from the Constitution. By 1936, therefore, the second policy, of which I spoke, the revolutionary policy of breaking with the Commonwealth, neared its climax. But the climax was delayed. Why?

The most important reason was concern for unity – an issue that was part external, part domestic. Might it not be that further advances towards republican sovereignty would impose a further barrier against national reunion? The question was debatable but at least its existence counselled caution. Another reason is often overlooked. Parallel with the renewed upsurge of Irish revolutionary nationalism there were, almost unnoticed in Ireland, constitutional developments in the Commonwealth which, while different in ultimate purpose, none the less in many respects kept pace with Irish advances. Let me give two illustrations. First, a simple matter of fact – it was not the Irish in November 1933 but the Canadians in May of that same year who were the first to abolish appeals in criminal cases to the Judicial Committee of the Privy Council. And secondly, the existence of a curious legal paradox. The Irish Courts, basing themselves on the Constitution of 1922 and the fundamental authority it gave to the provisions of the Treaty, as late as 1934, maintained that the Irish government were acting *ultra vires* in their constitutional reforms, because no power had been conferred upon them by which they were entitled to repeal the repugnancy clause in the Constitution. But what view was taken by the Judicial Committee of the Privy Council, the highest appellate tribunal in the Commonwealth, in London? They concluded in a judgement delivered in 1935, that the effect of the enactment of the Statute of Westminster, the legal charter of dominion liberties, was to remove the fetter that lay upon the Irish Free State legislature and that accordingly the Oireachtas had become free to pass legislation repugnant to imperial legislation – in which the Treaty had also been embodied – and noted that they had in fact done so. In other words, in British law, though not in Irish, Mr. de Valera's revolution was not in a narrow legal sense a revolution at all. He had done in the constitutional field what under British law he was entitled to do after 1931. It was J.H. Thomas who on this point had had the ground cut away from under his feet. In general, the fact that the overseas dominions were on the march towards independence within the Commonwealth helped to defer the day of Irish departure to independence outside it.

This was more strikingly illustrated late in 1936. In December of that year King Edward VIII, resolved to marry Mrs. Simpson against the advice of his government, abdicated. Under the Statute of Westminster this required action on the part of all dominion governments. What action was Mr. de Valera to take? He was at the time occupied in drafting a new Constitution. It would clearly have been at once more convenient and more logical to determine future relations with the Commonwealth after, and not before, the new Constitution was approved. But the Irish convenience and logic were minor casualties of royal impetuousity. The determination of external relations accordingly had to come before the Constitution. On the 11 December, 1936, Mr. de Valera introduced two pieces of legislation; a Constitution amendment bill and an External Relations Bill. He assured Mr. Cosgrave that they did not amount to a proposition to sever 'our connection with the states of the British Commonwealth'. But the first Act removed the King from the Legislature, the Executive and the Constitution generally; the second, the External Relations Act, proceeding from this elimination of the Crown in respect of internal government, allotted to it a narrowly defined place and limited functions in the external field. Diplomatic and consular representatives were to be appointed and every international agreement to be concluded on the authority of the Executive Council. But, so long as the Irish Free State was associated – and I quote because the precise wording is important – 'with the following nations, that is to say, Australia, Canada, Great Britain, New Zealand, and South Africa, and so long as the King recognized by those nations as the symbol of their co-operation continues to act on behalf of each of those nations (on the advice of the several governments thereof) for the purposes of the appointment of diplomatic and consular representatives and the conclusion of international agreements, the King so recognized may, and is hereby authorized to, act on behalf of Saorstát Eireann for the like purposes as and when advised by the Executive Council so to do.' It will be noticed that the Act was permissive and conditional. The procedure it outlined *might* be followed so long as the Commonwealth countries continued to co-operate and so long as they owed allegiance to the Crown. But permissive and conditional as it was, it acknowledged the role of the Crown in the Commonwealth without an explicit, or indeed implicit, recognition of Irish allegiance. The Constitution when enacted in 1937, effected no change, but in a somewhat ponderously phrased article sanctioned the regulation of external affairs in this or other ways as national interest might demand. Relations with Britain and the Commonwealth had thus been taken out of the Constitution, where Mr. de Valera felt that they had no place, and had become matters of external policy for the government of the day. This was the most significant development in the whole period.

Taken together the External Relations Act and the new Constitution destroyed the dominion settlement of 1921. The oath had gone, appeals to the Judicial Committee of the Privy Council had gone, the Governor-General had gone, the Crown had been taken out of the Constitution, the Constitution itself had been replaced by a Constitution republican in all but name with an elected President as its head and all that remained on paper of dominion status was the permissive procedure sanctioned by the External Relations Act. What was the British and Commonwealth reaction to revolutionary changes which had substituted for a dominion relationship the External association relationship that had been for so long Mr. de Valera's goal and which had been so vigorously repudiated by Lloyd George in 1921? The British Government considered the matter; they consulted with dominion governments and in agreement with them they issued a statement. The statement said that the British Government was prepared to treat the new Constitution 'as not affecting a fundamental alteration in the position of the Irish Free State as a member of the British Commonwealth of Nations'. As a piece of understatement this has its place in history. Well might one ask, well may Mr. de Valera have asked at the time, what then could affect a fundamental alteration? And yet the British reaction was eminently wise and statesmanlike. Finality was well avoided at the price of inconsistency transparently papered over. And Mr. de Valera for his part showed equal reluctance to burn his bridges behind him.

If indeed one looks at the situation in its widest context, here within a framework set by the details of past constitutional enactments, was an attempt to experiment in a new form of external relationship, starting on the one side from a foundation in republican nationalism and on the other from dominion precedents broadening down to national independence within a Commonwealth of Nations. The experiment may have been premature, the External Relations act may well have been, as its critics at home and overseas alleged, too much of an essay in political ingenuity to endure; but nonetheless many lessons were learned from it – not least by Jawaharlal Nehru, who concluded from it that it was in fact possible for an Indian Republic to remain a full member of the Commonwealth.

If relations with Britain and the Commonwealth dominated Irish thinking in this period there was one sufficient reason for it. First, it had to be shown and recognized in principle that Ireland was a sovereign state able to pursue an independent foreign policy and then particular restraints upon her freedom of action had to be considered. The first, freedom in principle, was securely established between 1926 and 1936; the second was deemed conditional upon the abrogation of the articles of the Treaty which gave to Britain the right, in time of peace, to harbour and other facilities in the Treaty ports and in time of war, or strained relations with a foreign power, such harbour and other facilities as the British Government might require for the defence of the British Isles. What would be the effect of the exercise of such rights by Britain in war time? Would a belligerent in such circumstances, to pose the crucial question, respect Irish neutrality? The question was one with which Mr. de Valera, to judge by his speeches, was increasingly preoccupied. He had been President of the Council of the League of Nations in 1932 and he was convinced even then that the testing time of the League had come. When, following Japanese invasions into Manchuria, Mussolini decided to invade Abyssinia, 'with Geneva, without Geneva, or against Geneva', Mr. de Valera warned the League: – 'Make no mistake, if on any pretext we were to permit the sovereignty of even the weakest state amongst us to be taken away, the whole foundation of the League would crumble into dust.' The Irish government supported sanctions. Opinion at home was troubled and divided. There was complaints moreover that Ireland was in this too closely associated with Britain – though as Mr. de Valera observed 'if your worst enemy happens to be going to Heaven by the same road as you are, you don't for that reason turn around and go in the other direction.' The League failed, Abyssinia was followed by the Rhineland; all the portents were of approaching war. What was a small state to do? Mr. de Valera, who was throughout his own Minister of External Affairs, was convinced, once collective security had broken down and the League had self-evidently failed, that for a small state there was only one course – neutrality. But was neutrality a possible policy with the Treaty ports in British hands? Mr. de Valera, as his exchanges with J.H. Thomas in 1932 testify, was at the least doubtful. But would the British be prepared to cede control on the eve of another World War? The answer, and it was a surprising one, was in the affirmative.

The 1938 Anglo-Irish agreement was in the nature of a package deal. It ended the economic war and it ceded British rights in the Treaty Ports to Ireland. This was very largely the doing of the British Prime Minister, Neville

Chamberlain. It is unfair to say, as his critics allege, that he was interested only in the appeasement of great and menacing totalitarian states. He was also interested in the appeasement of Ireland. He was concerned to conciliate, to end the bitterness of centuries. He felt that the return of the ports would further this broad political aim. He was assailed in the House of Commons by Winston Churchill. 'You are', he accused Chamberlain, 'casting away real and important means of security and survival for vain shadows and for ease.' But it would be nearer the truth to say that Chamberlain's action was prompted by faith and it is quite wrong to suppose that he disregarded altogether British strategic interests. On the contrary, he had, as we now know, a memorandum from the British Chiefs of Staff before him which did not on military grounds discourage the course, which for political reasons, he was resolved to pursue.

In the narrower context of Anglo-Irish relations it may be thought that the policy of appeasement bore lasting fruit. In the wider international context it ended in dismal failure. Hitler was not appeased. War came. Ireland adopted a policy of neutrality. She was enabled to do so in principle because the earlier redefining of dominion status coupled with the later vigorous reassertion of her national sovereignty had freed her from all constitutional obligation or other commitment to go to war when Britain was at war. She was enabled to do so in practice because the Anglo-Irish Agreement of 1938, in restoring the Treaty ports to Irish sovereignty had freed her from the serious risk of involvement by contingent liability. Since a decision on peace or war is the supreme test of sovereignty, it may be concluded, therefore, that the period 1926-39 is marked out in external relations as that in which the dominion that was the Irish Free State at its outset had become the state that exercised unquestioningly the final attributes of sovereignty at its close.

CATHOLICS IN NORTHERN
IRELAND, 1926–1939

David Kennedy

In 1926 there were 420,000 Catholics in Northern Ireland. They formed 33.5% of the total population and constituted the largest religious group, outnumbering the Presbyterians by about 30,000, and Protestant Episcopalians by 80,000.

This Catholic community was, and still is, composed mainly of small farmers, shopkeepers and unskilled labourers. It has a measurable share in the professions of medicine and law but its representation is negligible in the higher echelons of the Civil Service, public administration and the university. It plays a not unimportant part in the commercial life of Northern Ireland but it controls none of the heavy engineering and textile industries which are the basis of our economy. One Belfast daily paper, the *Irish News,* and several provincial papers represent and inform it. There are no Catholic landed gentry, though direct descendants of the old Catholic families, Gaelic and Norman, still live in territories over which their ancestors once ruled. They have given many leaders to the Church but they are almost without place in the civil Establishment.

The Catholic community is in the main of native Ulster stock, differing little in accent and habit from its Protestant neighbours. But there is also in Belfast a considerable element drawn from the south and west to provide the labour force for the great expansion of that city in the 1860's. Where the native-born Catholic was conciliatory and self-effacing the new arrivals were assertive, even obstreperous.

The Catholics of the North supported the Irish Parliamentary Party throughout the Home Rule agitation. The Party machine operated through the Ancient Order of Hibernians whose National President, Joseph Devlin, represented West Belfast at Westminster for many years. But like the rest of Ireland, the North was caught up in the wave of extreme nationalism which followed the Easter

Rising. The younger generation, both clergy and laity, became enthusiastic supporters of *Sinn Féin,* but the Primate, the bishops, the older priests and a large proportion of the electorate held aloof from, or were even hostile to, the new movement. In the landslide of the 1918 election, when the Irish Party retained only 6 seats in all Ireland, five of the six were in Ulster, and Eamon De Valera was roundly defeated by Joseph Devlin in West Belfast. Similar results followed in the election of 1921, held to elect members for the new parliament of Northern Ireland. This time Devlin's tenure of West Belfast was not contested by *Sinn Féin.*

This adherence to the Parliamentary Party was due in part to personal loyalty to Devlin, in part to the efficiency of the A.O.H. machine. In so far as it was anti-*Sinn Féin* it was because of the pragmatic Ulsterman's distrust of doctrinaire republicanism, and because he suspected that *Sinn Féin* knew little of the problems of the North. The Dáil debates on the Treaty, and the Civil War, confirmed the older generation in these attitudes. But the tide seemed to be flowing with the younger men. They were more vociferous, more energetic, and the I.R.A. was active in all the Ulster counties.

The Northern Nationalist's reaction to the Treaty and to the partition of Ireland embedded in it was compounded of shock, incredulity and resentment. *Sinn Féiners* did not want to believe that victory could hide such bitter fruit. They thought that the Northern Government would be unable to operate when its territory was cut down by the forthcoming Boundary Commission. In the last resort force of arms which had achieved so much would also win unity.

The existing cleavage in Ulster nationalism was little affected by the Civil War. Many leading I.R.A. officers accepted commissions in the Free State army. There were exceptions, of course – Joe McKelvey, afterwards executed, and Frank Aiken, were the most prominent among those who took the anti-treaty side. But the war was not fought in Ulster and we escaped the bitterness which has eaten into the lives of a generation of Irishmen. Instead, we had our own civil war, a war between Unionist and Nationalist made more hideous by the identification labels, 'Protestant' and 'Catholic', attached to each side.

Sectarian rioting had occurred in Derry, Belfast and other Northern towns in 1920. A force of Special Constabulary was recruited, ostensibly to preserve law and order. But attacks on Catholics continued throughout 1921 and 1922, and, after the setting-up of the Northern Government the Specials became a private army, recruited through the Orange Lodges and responsible only to the Executive. St Mary's Hall, the centre of Catholic diocesan organisation in Down & Connor, was commandeered to serve as their Headquarters. A Special Powers Act was passed in 1922 giving the Minister of Home Affairs extensive powers of arrest and internment without trial. All State and Local Authority employees were required to take an oath of allegiance to the Northern Government.

For the first year or two of the Government's existence Nationalists refused to cooperate with it. Their elected representatives refused to sit in Parliament. Catholic school managers refused to apply for grants. Catholics refused to sit on the Lynn Committee which remodelled the education system of Northern Ireland.

In the circumstances of the time these decisions were understandable. It was widely believed, and not by Nationalists only, that the new State would not last. In 1923 Devlin stated that he would await the outcome of the Boundary Commission before taking his seat in Parliament, even though the bishops were appealing for the resumption of constitutional opposition. It was unfortunate that no constructive criticism was heard from the Nationalist side during these early years, for the framework erected then in education and local government has endured to the present day and has operated to the grave disadvantage of the minority.

In 1925, when it was seen that there was to be no change of territory, Devlin and the Nationalist M.P. for Antrim took their seats. Three more M.P.'s followed in 1926. M.P's from the Border counties were more reluctant to come in, but by the end of 1927 Devlin led a party of ten in the House of Commons.

In their 1923 statement the Northern bishops had expressed their concern about the Government's treatment of Catholics. They stressed two points in particular. One was the abolition of proportional representation in local government elections and the rearrangement of constituencies to give control to Unionists. The other was the Education Act of 1923. Under this Act Education Committees were set up in all counties and county boroughs. These committees, under the control of the Local Authority, would maintain schools transferred to them by their former managers, build new ones where needed, and appoint teachers. The Act forbade the Education Authority to provide any religious education or to take religion into account in the appointment of teachers.

Schools not transferred were designated 'voluntary schools'. For them there was no building grant and nothing for upkeep and equipment. There was also a third type of school under what came to be known as a 'four-and-two' committee. The manager could nominate four persons (including himself and three other clerics, if desired) who would, with two nominees of the Local Authority, form a committee to manage the school. Certain expenses would then be met out of public funds. In view of the gerrymandering of Local Government electoral areas Catholics viewed any form of local control with suspicion, and in any case the financial inducements were not enticing. A few parish priests did accept this scheme, but it was rejected by the majority.

A formidable opposition to the Act was mounted by the Protestant churches. They demanded two major changes before they would agree to transfer their schools. Bible instruction was to be given, and steps were to be taken to ensure that Protestant children would be taught by Protestant teachers. These demands were conceded by the Amending Act, 1925, and further strengthened by the Amending Act, 1930.

When the latter Bill was going through Parliament Nationalist M.P.'s pleaded that, as the Act had been amended to suit Protestant demands, it should also be modified to suit Catholics. A deputation consisting of Bishop O'Kane of Derry, two M.P.'s, Devlin and Campbell, and the President of the Irish National Teachers' Organisation, presented the Catholic case to the Minister of Education. The Bishop of Down and Connor, Dr. Mageean, indicated in a public speech how the four-and-two committees might be made acceptable to Catholics, and the clergy of his diocese embodied his suggestions in definite proposals. Their main recommendation was 'that all matters relating to religious teaching, including the selection of the teacher, shall be subject to the control of those who represent Church interests on four-and-two committees. Their suggestions were rejected but, while giving in to Protestant demands on the one hand, the Government also agreed to pay 50% of the cost of building and equiping schools under managerial control.

The controversy over the Education Act embarrassed Devlin. He felt that in defending Catholic interests the Nationalist Party was being forced to play a sectarian role alien to his conception of nationalism. He had come into public life when as a young man he had had the temerity to challenge the Bishop and the Catholic Association in Belfast on this very point, and he reaffirmed his principles with passion now. 'I hate sectarianism as much as anybody. I fought against it when I was almost a boy, when I entered politics first. But anyone placed as I am, as the representative of my own people struggling to their feet and trying to hold their own, must be mixed up with all the tragedy of their position. But I never consented to be the leader of a Catholic Party and I never will consent.'

Time has shown that Devlin was mistaken in seeing the education controversy as a sectarian one. Both Catholics and Protestants were deeply concerned to keep religion in the schools. Both are still dissatisfied with the position, though for a time the Protestant Churches thought they had got what they wanted. In a normal State it might be possible to unite both Catholics and Protestants on this issue. In Northern Ireland it would still be impossible but, at least to-day, thanks to Pope John, it is conceivable. In the 1930's it was unthinkable. These were the years when Sir James

Craig declared 'This is a Protestant Parliament for a Protestant people'; when Cardinal MacRory offended many Christians by stating that the Protestant Churches did not form part of the true Church of Christ; when Sir Basil Brooke described Catholics as disloyal and advised Protestants not to employ them.

For about five years after Devlin's entry into the House of Commons there were hopes that better relations would develop between the two parties. He had launched the National League of the North pledged to constitutional opposition. 'There is not', he declared, 'and there is not going to be any attempt of any kind, much less a conspiracy, to force the people of Northern Ireland into a Dublin or any other parliament.' The Government made some conciliatory gestures. The first Lord Chief Justice, Sir Denis Henry, was a Catholic; so was the first Permanent Secretary to the Ministry of Education, Mr. Bonaparte Wyse. The Prime Minister, Sir James Craig, visited the Mater Hospital and met Devlin there to discuss extensions to the hospital. 'I was greatly impressed, with the place,' he wrote to his wife, 'it is beautifully run, as clean and bright as a new pin throughout, and everyone very pleasant and helpful.' Their discussions were fruitful and a piece of land was transferred from the adjoining Crumlin Road Jail to the Hospital.

But during these years it became apparent that the Government's weakness was on its own side of the House. It lost seven seats in the general election of 1925 to Independents, Labour and Farmers. In 1927, in divisions on the Intoxicating Liquor Bill its majority was at times as low as 8 and 9. In 1929 it took steps to deal with this situation by abolishing proportional representation at parliamentary elections. So the splinter groups were wiped out and it recouped its losses, but not at the expense of the Nationalists: they still returned 10 members. At the same time it noted that the simplest and surest way to rally Unionist voters was by identifying Catholicism with Nationalism and Nationalism with disloyalty. The slogan 'Not an Inch' proved to be the equilibrant of all the forces tending to disrupt the Unionist vote. But this slogan, and other anti-Catholic ones like those already quoted, inevitably widened the area of controversy.

The Nationalist position was also being undermined from within. Devlin, seeking lines of attack which would unite Catholic and Protestant, had launched a programme of public works to abolish slums and relieve unemployment. He soon found that the Government, even if willing, had not the power to raise the money to finance such schemes. Devlin never seemed to grasp the reality of the British Treasury's grip on Northern Ireland's economy. In the circumstances his genuine sympathy for the poor appeared to hostile critics as windy verbiage. Frustrated and ill, his resentment found expression in clashes with the Speaker, and was further increased when his long experience of parliamentary proceedure had to bow to the rulings of a novice. After one such clash he left the House, never to return. The new leader of the Party, T.J. Campbell, an able lawyer and former editor of the *Irish News,* lacked the power of leadership which the situation demanded. The Party threw up no tactician equal to Craig.

The situation was bedevilled by happenings south of the Border. In 1932 De Valera had assumed the reins of office in Dáil Eireann. He promptly abolished the oath of allegiance and released the republican prisoners. In the following year he contested and was returned for South Down in an election for the Northern Parliament. He had, of course, no intention of taking his seat. At the same time one of his followers, A.E. Donnelly, was elected as an Abstentionist in West Tyrone. Their intervention, and the apparent futility of Devlin's parliamentary group, strengthened the Northern Republicans. They decided to contest a number of seats in the 1935 Westminster election. Nationalists were in a dilemma. They had either to stand down or be blamed for splitting the vote. A Convention was called to meet in Omagh to decide on a course of action. While it was sitting Maurice Twomey, Chief of Staff of the I.R.A., was haranguing a crowd outside the hall. The Nationalists decided to withdraw and the Republicans contested and lost West Belfast, Down and Armagh to the Unionists. Only in Fermanagh-Tyrone were they successful. There, one of the newly-elected Abstentionists said: 'We held no election campaign. We simply issued a statement saying that if elected we would not go to Westminster.' And the other declared: 'I'm a farmer... being an M.P. doesn't interest me.'

An Act of 1934 made it impossible for Abstentionists to stand for the Northern Parliament. Unless a candidate declared his intention to take his seat if elected his nomination would be refused. But the virus of abstentionism infected the Nationalist M.P's. From 1934 onwards their attendance slackened, and after the general election of 1938 only Campbell and another member attended, and then only intermittently.

The 1930's were years of severe economic depression in Northern Ireland. The number of unemployed jumped from 35,000 in 1929 to 72,000 in 1930 and continued to rise until it reached 91,000 in 1938. A cut in outdoor relief rates in 1932 led to riots in which two people were killed. Agitators exploited the discontents of the times. A wing of the I.R.A. was avowedly communist in sympathy, and in a rail strike Protestant Trades Unionists allied with the I.R.A. committed acts of sabotage. In 1933 the Lenten pastorals of many bishops warned of the dangers of Communism, and in 1936 Bishop Mageean spoke in Belfast of Communism 'donning the cloak of patriotism'.

A wide street adjoining the Public Library in Royal Avenue, Belfast, gave space in those years for orators whose political spectrum ranged from pale pink to ultrared. I remember one of them addressing a crowd in words like these: 'If you took all the Orange sashes and all the Green sashes in Belfast and tied them round a ticket of loaves and threw them in the Lagan, the gulls, the common, ordinary sea-gulls, they'd go for the bread, but the other gulls – yous ones – yous'd go for the sashes every time'.

A vivid, homely and all too accurate picture.

In 1931 there were minor outbreaks of sectarian rioting in Armagh, Lisburn, Portadown and Belfast. In 1932 attacks were made in Ballymena, Larne and Portadown on pilgrims travelling to and from the Dublin Eucharistic Congress. In 1934 there were again minor incidents. And in July, 1935, there occurred the worst outbreak to disgrace the name of Belfast since 1922. Lord Justice Andrews summed up the damage at the City Commission in November: 11 murders and 2 attempted murders and in only 2 of the 13 had anyone been made amenable. 574 cases of criminal injuries to persons; 133 cases of arson; 367 cases of malicious damage. In only a few cases had it been possible to make any person responsible for the damage.

The Government refused an official inquiry into the riots asked for, in the House of Commons by T.J. Campbell, and outside the House by Bishop Mageean and Cardinal MacRory. Dr. Mageean carried his demand to England and the matter was raised in the British House of Commons, but the Prime Minister, Stanley Baldwin, blocked all attacks by the bland retort that the matter was one which came solely within the jurisdiction of the Northern Ireland Government.

These frustrated efforts, the economic distress of the times, the Government's inability to control its own extremists, its tenderness towards them compared with the vigour of its punishment for political opponents, all these combined to produce a smouldering resentment. Joseph Tomelty's play, *The End House* (produced at the Abbey Theatre, August, 1944) captures the bitter feelings of the decade 1930-40 and depicts the terror that darkened the lives of men and women in the little streets off the Falls Road. Dr. Mageean's Lenten Pastoral of 1938 gives expression to his feelings: 'Sixteen years ago the British Government forced a Parliament upon six of the nine counties of Ulster... The history of that Parliament is one long record of partisan and bigoted discrimination in matters of representation, legislation and administration... The British Government imposed this Parliament upon us and they are ultimately responsible for its acts. The Government that imposed it is the Government to abolish it.'

In 1934 the attention of the Council for Civil Liberties was called to the state of affairs existing in Northern Ireland. It sent a Commission of Inquiry to Belfast and its Report, published in 1936, summarises its findings as follows:

146

'Firstly, that through the operation of the Special Powers Act contempt has been begotten for the representative institutions of government.

Secondly, that through the use of Special Powers individual liberty is no longer protected by law, but is at the disposition of the Executive. This abrogation of the rule of law has been so practised as to bring the freedom of the subject into contempt.

Thirdly, that the Northern Government has used Special Powers towards securing the domination of one particular political faction and, at the same time, towards curtailing the lawful activities of its opponents... The Government's policy is thus driving its opponents into the way of extremists.

Fourthly, that the Northern Irish Government, despite its assurances that Special Powers are intended for use only against law-breakers, has frequently employed them against innocent and law-abiding people, often in humble circumstances, whose injuries, inflicted without cause or justification, have gone unrecompensed and disregarded.'

In the framework of this sober and damning indictment Bishop Mageean's outburst is understandable. His people were suffering. Parliamentary action had won no redress. He had intervened to protect them and had been fobbed off with a palpable evasion. But were they suffering as Catholics or as Nationalists? It was difficult to distinguish the two categories and, for the sufferer, irrelevant. But the question must be faced.

There was no persecution of the Catholic Church in Northern Ireland. In fact all through this decade it was showing obvious signs of vigorous and healthy growth. Three of the best known and most effective Catholic organisations in Ireland in modern times have had their origins in Down and Connor: the Catholic Truth Society, the Pioneer Association of the Sacred Heart, and the Apostolic Work Society. The last named which exists to send material aid to the foreign missions began in Belfast in 1923 with ten working girls as its first members. This cooperation between the workers and the Church continued to be a feature of Catholic Action throughout the 1930's.

One Belfast parish began to help the unemployed in the years of depression. Classes were organised, lectures and talks given, outings arranged to places of interest in the neighbourhood. A dramatic society presented plays in the Parochial Hall. Money was raised to send a number on a pilgrimage to Rome in the Holy Year, 1933.

On a wider scale a Catholic Social Conference in Belfast in 1937 pinpointed some of the evils of the time and suggested practical steps to remedy them. Two proved particularly effective. One was the establishment of a Social Service Bureau to deal with moneylenders and hire-purchase sharks preying on the poor, and to give legal aid to those in difficulties with landlords or Government bureaux. The other was the setting up of a Workers' College to give trade unionists a training in philosophy, economics and public administration.

Many other Catholic organisations were introduced into Northern Ireland during this period. The Legion of Mary and the CYMS came to Belfast in 1927; the Christian Arts Guild was founded here in 1931 and held its first annual Drama Festival in the following year. The Newman Society was inaugurated at Queen's University in 1930; the Irish Guild of St. Luke, St. Cosmas and St. Damien in 1932. With all this new activity superimposed on a substantial existing network of charitable organisations no wonder the official programme of the 31st Annual Conference of the Catholic Truth Society in Ireland, held in Belfast in 1934, claimed that 'the progress of the Church in this diocese has been very marked.'

Primarily much of this activity was due to an energetic bishop's implementation of the Church's programme of Catholic Action. But it was helped by the discrimination against Catholics practised by the Government, the Local Authorities and many public bodies. Forced back on their own resources Catholic men and women found outlets for their abilities in the service of their neighbours in the fellowship of the Church. The nature and scope of these activities, their impact on the Catholic community, the administrative ability of those who run them, show what Catholics can do when working as a coordinated unit. They are

148

the best retort to those apologists for discrimination who contend that Catholics, because of inferior education and lack of experience, are not suitable for top administrative posts. But the service they gave was a restricted one. It tended to ignore the wider implications of the answer to the question 'And who is my neighbour?' It tended to develop a spirit of mutual admiration and complacency. And it emphasised the apartheid mentality which is the curse of Northern Ireland.

In some parts of Belfast Catholics huddle together for mutual protection in little streets which abut on Protestant areas. During the 1935 riots the authorities erected barriers across the entrances to these streets to impede the progress of mobs bent on destruction. These tall, ugly structures of galvanised iron and timber were symbols of the ideological barriers which divide our community. They were removed after a few months. But their counterparts in our minds, built of fear, misunderstanding and prejudice, grew higher with the years and had become almost impregnable on the outbreak of war in 1939. The first major breach in them was made on the night of Easter Tuesday, 1941, by the blast of exploding German bombs.

THE POLITICAL SCENE IN
NORTHERN IRELAND, 1926–1937

Professor J. L. McCracken

I want to talk to you about political events in Northern Ireland between 1926 and 1937. Let me say right away that these dates have less significance for the North than they have for the Irish Free State. In a sense nothing out of the ordinary happened: there was no change of government, no new parties emerged, no important constitutional issues were raised. The policies which had been initiated in the early days of the state were pursued with little modification. The men who dominated the political scene remained very much the same. And yet when all this is said it is possible to ascribe a definite character to these years; they can, I think, be regarded as the years of consolidation.

By this time Northern Ireland had survived two formidable threats to its existence. The first was the 'Troubles' – the guerilla war and the reprisals – which threatened to engulf the new state in anarchy. To overcome this crisis the Northern government had relied in part on the British army. But since there were doubts in the minds of the Ulster leaders about the extent to which they could trust the British government they had also established a regular police force and had built up a special constabulary to constitute what Sir James Craig called 'our force, which must be called a defence force, against our enemies.' The other threat which had hung over the heads of the Northern government for even longer was the Boundary Commission. As early as May 1922 Craig pointed out that the arrangement for a commission had been entered into behind his back and he made it clear that he would have nothing to do with it. 'What we have now, we hold,' he said, 'and we will hold against all combinations.' When the Commission was on the point of becoming a reality he again revealed his sense of insecurity and his reservations about the British government's reliability by drawing attention to the possibility that if the Commission's report did not satisfy the Irish Free State it might apply the screw on the British government and Ulster might be deprived of so much of her territory that the Northern government would find it impossible to carry on. Whatever the outcome, he announced that if the findings were unacceptable to Northern Ireland he would resign as prime minister and put himself at the disposal of the people to defend any territory which they considered had been unfairly transferred. In the light of these fears and uncertainties it is not surprising that Craig should have spoken of his deep thankfulness and relief on the conclusion of the Boundary Agreement which, as you know, left the boundary between Northern Ireland and the Irish Free State unchanged.

The strain and insecurity of these early years served to confirm the Unionist leaders in their determination to maintain the Northern state intact. Gone were the days when they had stressed the sacrifice they had made in agreeing to self-government against their wishes. Now that they had, as Craig put it, 'got the ship safely steered to port' they were confident in their ability to keep it afloat. And they had no longer any reason for entertaining suspicions about British intentions towards Ulster. They were at last free to set about consolidating their position, freed from the threat of imminent destruction.

Amongst the minority in the North, too, things were happening which pointed to the consolidation of the Northern state. They had originally taken the line of non-co-operation. At one point a group of teachers in Tyrone even announced that they would not accept their salaries from the Northern government. While there was still doubt about the future of Northern Ireland the anti-partition M.Ps. refused to take their seats in parliament. But in 1925 two of the Nationalists came in and by 1927 they had been joined by the other eight, leaving only two irreconcilable Republicans outside. This opened the way to Nationalist representation in the senate because apart from the two ex-officio members – the Lord Mayor of Belfast and the Mayor of Londonderry – the senators were elected by the members of the house of commons on a system of proportional representation. In the parliament which assembled after the general election of 1929 three Nationalists were returned to the senate. At first the Nationalist M.Ps were not organized as a party – Mr. Joseph Devlin, the ablest of them, said he had no ambition to lead anyone – and they declined to act as the official opposition. Though they persisted in their refusal when the Labour party formally renounced the role of opposition they did take a step towards organization when the National League was formed in May 1928. Its aims were to achieve the national unity of Ireland, to demand justice for Nationalists and to foster cooperation amongst all creeds and classes. Devlin struck a conciliatory note when he said that things were changing: there was a fresher atmosphere in Belfast; the masses of the people were now friendly; politics were no longer a cause for men hating each other. And he took occasion to announce that there was no conspiracy to force the people of Northern Ireland into a Dublin parliament. Other Nationalist leaders, too, showed a disposition to make the best of what was, to them, a bad business. Mr. McAllister said in the house 'I realize today that the partition of Ireland is an accomplished fact' and Mr. Cahir Healy told a meeting of Fermanagh Nationalists that the Unionists were trying to draw a red herring with regard to the Nationalists wanting to abolish the Belfast parliament. 'Many of us,' he said, 'would be prepared to leave them their parliament in Belfast for as long as it was considered necessary for local purposes. I quite see that the existence of four provincial parliaments in Ireland would not be a bar to national unity but on the contrary might make for efficiency.'

The Nationalist members for a time played an active role as critics of the government and as champions of the rights of their community. Until his death in 1934 Devlin was one of the outstanding members of the house of commons. An experienced parliamentarian, an eloquent speaker, a thorough Ulsterman, he and Craig were worthy protagonists and there was a strong bond of respect and esteem between them. Devlin and his colleagues did not labour in vain. Apart from their contribution to the return to normality they had positive achievements to their credit as when they induced the government to agree in 1930 that non-transferred schools should get grants of 50% of the cost of building.

But the abstention issue was by no means settled. The Nationalist M.Ps. themselves periodically withdrew from the house and the Republicans never took their seats. These internal dissensions weakened the effectiveness of the opposition and it was in an effort to remedy the situation – a not very successful one as it proved – that a new organization was set up in 1936. This was the Irish Union Association which was established in Belfast after a convention attended by representatives of all minorities in Northern Ireland. Its aim was to bridge the gulf between Nationalist, Republican and Fianna Fáil supporters in the province, especially over the question of abstention.

The truth is the parliamentary representatives of the minority had put themselves in an impossible position. Whether they were, like Devlin, in the tradition of the old home rule party of John Redmond or whether they were out and out Republicans their basic aim was to secure a united Ireland. In other words they wanted to undermine the regime that had been established in the North by the act of 1920. That being so they could not play the role of an opposition in the traditional British manner; the relations between government and opposition which existed in Britain could not exist in the North even though the Northern parliament was modelled on the British one. More than that, they drew their support exclusively from the Catholic part of the population just as the Unionists did, probably equally exclusively, from the Protestant part. So to the fundamental division on the political issue of a united Ireland versus a partitioned one was added a pretty clear cut religious division also. Finally, they could never hope to be other than an opposition; they could never look forward to assuming office. A persistent charge in Nationalist circles was that the Unionists had gerrymandered the constituencies so as to deprive them of their fair share of repre-

153

sentation in the house. They pointed out that the abolition of P.R. in local government elections had cost them the control of bodies like the Tyrone County Council and Derry Corporation where they had a majority. The Unionist reply was that they had only themselves to blame: when a commissioner had been sent round the province to map out local government constituencies they boycotted his work and refused to allow anyone to submit evidence to him. However that may be, the position in parliamentary elections is clear enough: so long as the constitutional problem remained basic to Irish political life, so long as they were the representatives of the Catholic minority, no rearrangement of the constituencies that could have been devised would have brought them anywhere within reach of constituting a majority in the house.

Certain consequences followed from this situation. It enabled – indeed it almost obliged – Unionists to appropriate loyalty and good citizenship to themselves and to use the national flag as a party emblem; it led, at least in the popular mind, to the identification of Catholicism with hostility to the state; it detracted from the effectiveness of opposition criticism of the government even on issues which had no bearing on the constitutional question; and it encouraged irresponsibility, rashness and a narrow sectarian approach on the part of some Nationalist members. The Nationalists would undoubtedly have been more weighty as an opposition, they would probably have better served the interests of the minority and indeed of the whole community, they might have contributed to a better understanding between North and South if they had been prepared, even as a short-term policy, to accept fully and frankly the constitutional position as they found it – as De Valera did when he entered the Dáil in 1927.

Nationalist participation in political life was not unwelcome to the Unionists. Mr. J.C. Davison was expressing a fairly generally held view when he said in the commons 'We are glad to see them coming in and taking part in the proceedings of this assembly.' No doubt this attitude owed much to the assured majority which the Unionists enjoyed. A feature of these years was the uniform success

154

of the Unionists at general elections, the continuity of service among the members and, in consequence, the unchanging social pattern in the two houses. Two general elections fell within the period we are considering – in 1929 and 1933 – and two just outside the period – in 1925 and 1938. From all of them the Unionist party emerged with an overwhelming and virtually unchanged majority. From 1929 onwards they held 37, 36 and 39 seats in a house of 52 members. Only in 1925 when the election was conducted under a system of proportional representation did their numbers sink as low as 32 but this is less significant than it might seem for there were 5 independents in that parliament whose sympathies lay with the Unionists on the constitutional issue. Not only were the Unionists returned in overwhelming numbers but a high proportion of them did not even have to contest their seats: in 1933, for example, 27 of the 36 Unionist members were returned unopposed. And not only did the same party dominate the electoral scene but the same individuals tended to be re-elected. Of the 52 members who were sitting in the house of commons in 1927, 28 or 54% were still members in 1936 and, what is more, 21 of them – 40% of the house – had been members since the establishment of the parliament in 1921. At government level we find the same continuity. In 1927 Lord Craigavon had been prime minister since the setting up of the state and he was to remain in office until his death in 1940. Only one member of his first cabinet had resigned by 1927 and three of his original five colleagues were still in office in 1936.

It follows that there was no appreciable change in the class and occupational structure of parliament. Lawyers and company directors, including some of the leading linen lords, made up nearly half the membership of the house of commons in 1927. A sprinkling of doctors, a couple of leading newspaper editors and various types of businessmen filled most of the remaining places. The striking thing is that apart from the landed gentry who were also usually great industrialists agriculture was so ill represented.

Since the senate was only a shadow of the commons most

of what has been said about the Unionist M.Ps is true of senators also. And it is equally applicable to the anti-partition members – the group of Nationalists, varying from 9 to 12 and the one or two Republicans who consistently abstained. They too neither lost nor gained much ground and they had their long-service members as well.

Now, as I said a few minutes ago the Unionist leaders were quite happy to have the Nationalist members in the house. What was distinctly unacceptable was to have any deviationist tendencies amongst their own supporters. This was one of the major problems that had to be solved as part of the process of consolidation. In the early years various pressure groups caused embarrassment to the government. In 1925 the parliamentary secretary to the ministry of Home Affairs lost his seat to a representative of the Unbought Tenants. The Protestant churches and the Orange Order were agitating for an amendment to the Education Act of 1923 and temperance reformers, strongly backed by sections of the Protestant clergy were pressing for a measure of local option. The Local Optionists carried their campaign to the length of putting up candidates in opposition to official Unionists in the general election of 1929. The Unionist party saw the danger in such appeals as 'What will it profit you if you gain a political victory and lose your own son or daughter through drink?' and it called for a closing of the ranks. Craigavon himself denounced them in no uncertain terms. 'They need not ride off under any plea that they are as good Unionists as the rest of us,' he said. 'They cannot do that. How can a man be a loyal Unionist if he attempts to stab the leaders of Ulster, through trying times, in the back.' And the *Belfast Newsletter* put the party case in a nutshell when it said: 'A majority composed even in part of men who put subordinate issues in front of their Unionism will not suffice.'

These were the men the prime minister had in mind, and not the Nationalists, when he decided to abolish proportional representation in parliamentary elections, except for the university seats. In his opinion P.R. submerged and clouded the issue. 'What I hold is, if the Ulster people are ever going – and pray God they may not – into a Dublin parliament I say let the people understand that they are voting to go into a Dublin parliament and not go in by any trick of a complicated system such as P.R.' Although P.R. had been abandoned in local government elections in 1921 and had been under attack from the Unionists ever since, it was only in 1929 as part of the process of consolidation that P.R. was abolished for parliamentary elections. The change to single-member constituencies had little effect on the opposition. Craigavon was right when he said: 'There are really underlying everything two active, alert, vigorous parties in Ulster... one for the Empire, the other for an all-Ireland parliament in Dublin.' As things were there was no place for the Labour party or for independents. Labour had won 3 seats under P.R. in 1925; in later elections it got one or two and there is no reason to believe that its position would have improved if P.R. had been retained, certainly not so long as they maintained an equivocal attitude on the constitutional question. As for the Nationalists their parliamentary strength remained virtually unchanged. What the abolition of P.R. did was to prevent splinter groups of Unionists from securing separate parliamentary representation. The Unionist party continued to be a broad-based organization and the Northern government remained particularly sensitive to back-bench opinion but since 1929 differences of opinion have usually been thrashed out within the party circle and when a dissentient group like the Progressive Unionists took the electoral field in 1938 they made no showing whatever.

As Northern Ireland found its feet in these years its place in the United Kingdom and its relations with Britain took clearer shape. The Boundary Agreement put an end to Unionist suspicions of British intentions; amendments in the financial arrangements between the two areas were worked out; and as the legislative output of the Northern parliament grew the development of the 'step by step' policy became evident. Northern Ireland was entitled to thirteen seats in the imperial parliament at Westminster and in the early years a good many of them were occupied by Unionist members of the Northern Ireland parliament. But at the general election of 1929 Craigavon imposed a veto on this arrangement with the object of ensuring that the Northern representatives would be in a better position to support the Conservatives at Westminster. His chief whip, Captain Herbert Dixon, was the only Unionist left with a seat in both houses.

In the economic sphere these were years of persistent depression and unemployment. The two great Ulster industries, linen and shipbuilding, were in decline and agriculture was hard hit by the industrial depression at home and in Britain. The government attempted to stimulate 'by granting loans for capital undertakings, by offering inducements to new industrial ventures, by encouraging the home consumption of Ulster goods and by marketing legislation designed to promote agriculture.' But its efforts were to little effect. Unemployment rose from 13% in 1927 to a peak of 28% in 1931 and was still as high as 23% in 1936.

A by-product of the high unemployment was a resurgence of sectarian strife and a renewal of the campaign of violence. Interference with an Orange demonstration at Cootehill on 13 August 1931 sparked off a series of reprisals. Disturbances in succeeding years culminated in the summer of 1935 in serious rioting in Belfast in which a number of people were killed. It is a measure of the extent to which stability had been achieved in these years that the campaign of violence was no more than a nuisance – no longer a danger – and that the riots were the last to get out of hand.

There are other ways in which these are marked as years of consolidation. In 1926 it was decided to establish an Inn of Court for Northern Ireland and in 1933 the Law Courts Building was opened in Belfast. Even more impressive as physical evidence of a separate regime in the North was the erection of Stormont. Its significance was fully appreciated: just before the laying of the foundation stone in 1928 the minister of finance, Mr. Pollock, said that he regarded the function 'as the outward and visible proof of the permanence of our institutions; that for all time we are bound indissolubly to the British crown'. The opening of the building in November 1932 was the occasion for a great Unionist demonstration – but the Nationalist M.Ps took no part in the ceremony as a protest against partition.

The final point I want to make is that the course of events in the Irish Free State in these years contributed not a little to the consolidation of the regime in the North. One clause in the Boundary Agreement of 1925 had provided for periodical meetings between the governments of the Irish Free State and of Northern Ireland to consider certain matters of common concern. No such meeting ever took place; neither government was sufficiently master in its own house to risk the possible domestic repercussions. The North was suspicious of the Free State government's intentions and concerned about the existence of the dissentient groups. That is what justified, in Unionist eyes, the retention of the Special Powers Act. This act had originally been passed in 1922 at the height of the 'Troubles' to strengthen the hands of the civil authorities. It was renewed from year to year until 1928 when, after an acrimonious debate in the commons, it was re-enacted for five years. Sir Dawson Bates defended the government's action on the ground that there were forces at work in the province and elsewhere which would plunge them into a welter of bloodshed if there was the slightest relaxation of the law. In 1933 the Act was made permanent and once again a member is found alleging that the whole trouble came from outside.

The change of government in the Free State in 1932 was followed by the resurgence of old and the appearance of new extra-parliamentary groups bitterly hostile to the North. More than that, the new government's policy of dismantling the Anglo-Irish Treaty and of pressing the question of partition confirmed the Northern government's worst fears. At a very early stage in the Anglo-Irish dispute Lord Craigavon made his position clear. 'We here in the Ulster area stand today exactly where we stood through the past eleven years. The result of the general election of 1933 enabled him to claim that this attitude had been endorsed by the people. When the new parliament assembled he applied to the Ulster situation the same doctrine of self-determination as Mr. de Valera had enunciated in support of his government's stand. 'We here in Ulster', he said,

159

'have a moral and constitutional right to remain in the closest association with Great Britain and the Empire. That is a matter for us, and not a matter of grievance for any other one of the states. It is for the Ulster people to decide what their association with Great Britain and the Empire will be. The citizens of Northern Ireland are not going to be a slave people under a Free State parliament, and still less in an Irish Republic, and they are not content to have any dictation from any such government'. As an indication of the hardening in the Unionist position mention may be made of an act of 1934 which extended the period of residence from three to seven years as a qualification for voting in parliamentary elections and which required candidates at their nomination to make a declaration of their intention to take their seats. The first provision was aimed at the people 'who come in here to help to break the last link between Great Britain and Ireland,' the second at the Republican abstentionists. The activities and the pronouncements of the extra-parliamentary groups in the Free State stoked the fires of resentment but so too did the raising of the partition question at the successive conferences between the Irish and British governments between 1932 and 1938. When the Anglo-Irish dispute was in its closing stages, with partition still on the agenda, the Northern government again went to the polls on the old issue. The result was a notable victory. In 1921 the Unionists had held 40 seats, in 1938 they won 39. Craigavon claimed that the election had, in his own words, 'vindicated the deep-seated resolve in the hearts of all loyal Ulstermen and women that come what may our position within the United Kingdom and the Empire must remain unchanged.'

TOWARDS THE NEW CONSTITUTION

Vincent Grogan

The period of twenty years beginning in 1916 is of perhaps unique importance in the history of our country. In the first decade of the period national freedom had been asserted, the Irish Republic proclaimed, fought for in arms and ratified in blood. Compromise, dictated by military necessity, had resulted in the Treaty Settlement of 1921, establishing, in place of the Republic, the Irish Free State. But those who had fought, as they believed, for a living Republic, had pitched their claims too high to permit of conventional acceptance of such a compromise, and the agony of decision had provoked a civil war. By the middle of 1923, the civil war was over and the Irish Free State had been stabilised, but a large minority of its citizens were still unreconciled to its very existence.

Dorothy Macardle, in her work, *The Irish Republic* was moved to write: 'Ireland was partitioned and impoverished, her people embittered by disappointment, divided and distraught by a half-measure of freedom and exhausted by war.' Many would object to the term 'half-measure' but few could cavil at the general picture. It is in this setting that the subsequent development of the Irish Free State has to be considered.

The fundamental law of the Irish Free State was the Anglo-Irish Treaty. That is the only categorical statement that can be made about the legal basis of the State, as to which there are, otherwise, irreconcilable differences of opinion. Within the limits of this lecture one can only give a brief outline of the opposing views.

An election was held in June, 1922, in the twenty-six counties for a House of Parliament to which the Provisional Government (established under the Treaty) would be responsible. This election was held in pursuance of the British statute (the Irish Free State Agreement Act, 1922) which had given the Treaty the force of law. The Second Dáil Eireann – which, by a small majority, had accepted the Treaty – decreed that these elections should be treated as elections for the Third Dáil, and that six-county constituencies, in which there would be no election, should continue to be represented by their sitting deputies.

The Provisional Parliament was summoned under the authority of the British statute and not under the decree of the Dáil. It enacted a measure entitled The Constitution of the Irish Free State (Saorstát Eireann) Act, 1922. In the Preamble to this Act it described itself, comprehensively if ambiguously, as 'Dáil Eireann, sitting as a Constituent Assembly in this Provisional Parliament.'

The use of the title, Dáil Eireann, was no doubt intended to give an appearance of Republican legality and continuity, but it was clearly not the Third Dáil. It had not been convened as such, and the Second Dáil had not been dissolved. Its claim to be a Constituent Assembly afterwards found uncritical support in the judgment of Chief Justice Kennedy in the leading case of *The State (Ryan) v. Lennon,* decided in 1934.

The Constituent Act, so-called, declared the Constitution, set out in a Schedule, to be the Constitution of the Irish Free State. Any provision of the Constitution, or any amendment to it, was declared void so far as it was repugnant to the Treaty.

The British view was that the British statute from which alone the Provisional Parliament received its authority gave it no power to enact a Constitution. The United Kingdom Parliament accordingly enacted The Irish Free State Constitution Act, 1922. This appended the Irish measure as a Schedule, and declared the Constitution scheduled to that measure to be the Constitution of the Irish Free State, subject, again, to the overriding authority of the Treaty.

The Treaty gave Ireland 'the same constitutional status in the Community of Nations known as the British Empire as the Dominion of Canada, the Commonwealth of Australia, the Dominion of New Zealand, and the Union of South Africa, with a Parliament having powers to make laws for the peace, order and good government' of the State. This gave her virtually complete internal self-government. The decisions of her Supreme Court were, however, subject to review by the Judicial Committee of the Privy Council. She had no power to make laws having extra-territorial effect; her citizens were subjects of the Imperial Crown, bound to it by a common allegiance, her members of parliament oath-bound to be faithful to H. M. King George V, his heirs and successors. The King was represented by a Governor-General, who was the nominee of the British Government. He was invested with certain powers of reservation and disallowance of Bills, powers which, though long dormant, could not be said to be extinct.

A further, and more serious, disability lay in the conduct of foreign affairs. The United Kingdom Government could commit the whole Empire to international obligations – and even to war – although, by 1926, a convention had been established that such powers would not be exercised except after consultation with – and perhaps, but not certainly, with the consent of – the Dominions.

Of all these marks of subordination, that which hurt most was allegiance to the British Crown, and more particularly the oath of allegiance which every member of the Oireachtas was required to take. This had been, in the words of one of the Treaty signatories, Eamon Duggan, 'the most thorny subject in all the negotiations'. Insistence upon it – and not Partition – had been the chief cause of the 'split' which eventually resulted in civil war. The members of the Republican Dáil had already taken an oath to defend the Republic and, in the anti-Treaty view, passionately held in the Treaty debates, they could not absolve themselves from it. Moreover, the National Executive of the Volunteers (later known as the Irish Republican Army) had insisted upon the Dáil deputies taking this oath to the Republic, which they themselves had already taken, as an essential pre-condition to accepting the jurisdiction of the Dáil.

On October 25, 1922, the day on which the Provisional Parliament passed the Constituent Act, a secret meeting of the Republican members of the Second Dáil was held in Dublin. They declared that they now represented the Republican Dáil, the pro-Treaty members having abandoned the Republic, and re-appointed Mr. de Valera President of the Republic.

This stand upon principle could, however, be little more than a gesture. It soon became clear that they could not hope to carry a war-weary country with them. Mr. de Valera eventually came to the conclusion that the de facto existence of the Irish Free State would have to be accepted.

Defeated by a narrow majority on this issue at a meeting of the Sinn Féin party, of which he was still President, he resigned from that party and founded Fianna Fáil. The new party would contest Free State elections; its deputies would not take the oath but if and when they secured a majority they would demand admittance as of right. This plan was frustrated by Mr. Cosgrave's Government when, in August, 1927, an Electoral Bill was introduced, requiring candidates to swear before nomination an affidavit of intention to take their seats and to take the oath, if elected, and providing for forfeiture of their seats if they failed to do so.

In the meantime, it was being bruited about by some sitting members of the Dáil that, in reality, no oath was administered, that deputies were merely asked to *sign* a declaration in the terms of the oath. In their dilemma, the Fianna Fáil deputies decided to test this. They met together on 10th August, 1927, and issued a signed declaration to the press, announcing that they intended to present themselves at the 'Clerk's Office of the Free State Dáil 'for the purpose of complying with the provisions of Article 17 of the Constitution', by inscribing their names in the book kept for the purpose, among other signatures appended to the required formula.' The statement went on to say that they would regard the declaration so signed as 'an empty formality'.

Mr. de Valera then led his deputies to the office of the Clerk, Colm O Murchadha. A book was indicated to him, on the open page of which was, apparently, a declaration that the undersigned subscribed to the terms of the oath. On the book lay a Testament, which he removed, placing it on a nearby chair. He then addressed the Clerk in Irish, as follows: 'Ba mhaith liom a chur in iúl duit nach bhfuil mé le mionn a thógaint, ná aon gheallúint dílseachta do Rí Shasana a thabhairt – ná d'aon chomhacht taobh a-muigh de mhuinntir na hÉireann. Táim ag cur m'ainmse annseo chun cead fháil dul isteach imeasc na dteachta a toghadh ag muinntir na hÉireann, agus bíodh fhios agat nach bhfuil aon bhrí eile leis an rud atá á dhéanamh agam'. ('I wish to inform you that I am not going to take an oath or to give any promise of allegiance to the King of England or to any power apart from the Irish people. I am putting my name here to obtain permission to enter among the deputies elected by the Irish people. Understand that there is no other meaning to what I am doing.') He and his followers then signed the book, and were permitted to take their seats.

There was much misunderstanding, and indeed misrepresentation, then and for long afterwards as to what had transpired. It was asserted that they had taken the oath with a mental reservation, and had declared the oath so taken to be an 'empty formula'. It is clear from the evidence that no oath was taken. A statement made at the time by the late Archbishop Mannix is of interest: 'There is no oath' he stated 'because there is no *intention* to invoke God as witness, and there is no deception because Mr. de Valera declared from the housetops that he has *no* intention of invoking God to declare allegiance to a foreign King.'

With extraordinary prescience, William Magennis, Professor of Metaphysics in University College, Dublin, had foreseen the possibility of this solution in 1922. Speaking in the debate on the draft Constitution on October 3, 1922, he said 'It would be quite easy to have the oath written down as a formula to which members may sign their names in an official book.'

The Electoral Act, which had precipitated the decision, was passed in the following November. It was in force for the purposes of the next general election, held in 1932. There seems, however, to have been a tacit agreement all round to treat it as a dead letter. Its implementation was left to the constituency returning officers and, while some candidates may have produced a signed form of affidavit, there is no evidence that anyone was in fact obliged to swear one. The actual procedure of 'compliance' with the requirement of Article 17 was the same as that followed in 1927.

Mr. Cosgrave, first President of the Executive Council of the Irish Free State, was defeated in the 1932 elections and succeeded by Mr. de Valera. The outgoing Government, in collaboration with other members of the Commonwealth in a series of Dominion Conferences, had substantially vindicated Michael Collins's claim that the Treaty, if it did not give full freedom, gave freedom to achieve it. The process, already more fully described by Dr. Nicholas Mansergh in an earlier lecture in this series, resulted in the State's achieving coequal status with the United Kingdom as a member of the British Commonwealth of Nations. The king remained as head of the State but he now functioned, so far as Irish affairs were concerned, entirely at the will of the Irish Government.

The new Government's first constitutional measure was the Constitution (Removal of Oath) Bill which proposed to delete the oath and repeal words which required amendments of the Constitution to be within the terms of the Treaty. It proposed also to repeal section 2 of the Constituent Act which gave the Treaty the force of law and declared amendments of the scheduled Constitution in conflict with it to be void.

On the theory consistently advanced by the previous Free State administration this last amendment was clearly invalid: the Oireachtas only had power to amend the Constitution; the Constituent Act, which gave overriding authority to the Treaty, was the work of the Constituent Assembly and could not be amended at all. On the British view, however, that Act itself derived its validity from a British statute, and the Statute of Westminster, 1931, had given the Oireachtas the legal right to override any British statute, and even to abrogate the Treaty itself.

Mr. de Valera had little regard for either theory. He claimed to be acting in accordance with a popular mandate and, whatever constitutional lawyers might argue, that was enough for him.

The British Government, for its part, far from recognising the logic of the situation, now sent a note protesting that the measure was contrary to the terms of the Treaty. The Seanad rejected the Bill which was therefore held up until 1933.

The constitutional 'revolution' proceeded nonetheless. Further Acts were passed in November, 1933, eliminating the Governor-General's discretionary functions and abolishing the right of appeal to the Privy Council.

In 1935 a new Citizenship Act was enacted, regulating citizenship for all purposes, international as well as domestic. The British Government declined to recognise the new Irish citizenship as exclusive and universal. Irish citizens resident in Britain, or elsewhere, were still regarded therefore as British subjects. This attitude had serious practical consequences in 1939 when Britain went to war and Ireland maintained neutrality.

The next change in constitutional status was precipitated by the British abdication crisis of December, 1936, when Edward VIII determined to relinquish the throne. Mr. de Valera took advantage of the occasion to convert the relationship of the country to the Commonwealth to that proposed by him in 1921, namely, external association.

A constitutional amendment was passed on December 11, 1936 (the day after the King had signed his 'declaration of abdication'), deleting all references to King and Governor-General, thus depriving the Crown of all internal executive and other functions. On the same day, the British Parliament, acting with the consent and on behalf of the other Dominions, passed an Act declaring a demise of the Crown in favour of the next in line of succession. That statute had no effect in the Irish Free State where, accordingly, King Edward VIII continued for the time being to reign while his brother reigned in the rest of the Commonwealth as George VI.

On the following day, December 12, the Oireachtas passed the Executive Authority (External Relations) Act, 1936. This Act 'accepted' the king's abdication for the Irish Free State, but did not enthrone any successor. Instead, it merely authorised the king recognised by the other Dominions as the 'symbol of their cooperation' to act on behalf of the State for certain diplomatic and treaty-making purposes on the advice of the Irish Government.

The Irish Free State had ceased to be one of His Majesty's Dominions. It had become an Associated State, republican in form, without a titular Head.

Kevin O'Higgins had said in the Constitution debates (18 September, 1922): 'There is no constitutional hybrid between a Republic and a Monarchy. Mr. de Valera had thought that he had begotten one, but nobody loved it and he abandoned it himself.' Mr. O'Higgins's opinion was premature: it had not been abandoned; its parturition had taken fourteen years. Mr. de Valera had now brought forth – and the child was accepted by the other members of the Commonwealth. It was, no doubt, true that nobody loved it: Mr. Costello certainly did not, for he abandoned it finally with the repeal of the External Relations Act by the Republic of Ireland Act, 1948.

We have so far been considering the growth of the country's status to full international maturity. It remains to examine the changes that occurred over the same period in the internal structure of the Constitution. Here, regrettably, the story is not of growth but of deformity. For most of the retrogressive constitutional changes that occurred in those years responsibility must be laid at the door of those who engaged in unconstitutional activities.

The Constitution of 1922 contained a solemn declaration of individual freedom: 'The liberty of the person is inviolable and no person shall be deprived of his liberty save in accordance with law'. Freedom of expression of opinion was guaranteed. Habeas corpus procedure was written into the Constitution to assure personal liberty under the law. Provision was made for direct participation of the people in law-making, whether by referendum or by the initiation by the people themselves of legislative measures. They did not, however, long survive. The Referendum and Initiative were both abolished in 1928 in order to frustrate an attempt to use them for the elimination of the oath. The guarantee of personal liberty soon gave way under pressure of the civil war and subsequent political violence. A Public Safety (Emergency Powers) Act, 1923, was the first of a series of measures providing for detention without trial, and for military tribunals for the trial, if trial was expedient, of political offenders. These various measures were upheld by the courts as being 'in accordance with law', leaving personal liberty at the mercy of the legislature.

There were short periods when none of these measures was actually in force. One such brief spell came to an end when Kevin O'Higgins was assassinated on July 10, 1927. Again, there was a lull from 1929 to 1931, when a fresh outbreak of illegal activity provoked the passing of the most comprehensively repressive measure of all, the Constitution (Amendment No. 17) Act, which inserted into the very forefront of the Constitution, as Article 2A, a whole code of repression, including the establishment of a military tribunal to try a wide range of offences. This tribunal was given the power to substitute, for the punishment provided by law for an offence, any greater punishment (including the penalty of death) if in the opinion of the tribunal it was 'necessary or expedient' to do so. One of the offences scheduled was possession of a firearm without a licence. There was no appeal from the verdict of this tribunal.

This Article remained in the Constitution until the Constitution itself was repealed in 1937. Although its passage was opposed by Mr. de Valera, his Government in its turn found it necessary to make use of it. Having suspended its operation in March, 1932, they brought it back into force in August, 1933.

Chief Justice Kennedy, in his judgment in *Ryan's Case,* expressed the opinion that Article 2A was unconstitutional, as being contrary to natural law, but he was overruled by the other two judges. Two further important changes must be noted. The Constitution of 1922 was intended ultimately to be a rigid one – amendable only by a popular referendum – after an initial period of eight years, during which it was to be amendable by ordinary legislation. In 1929 this period was enlarged, by ordinary legislation, to sixteen years. This amendment was upheld by the majority of the judges in *Ryan's Case*. It followed from this that the Oireachtas could prolong this 'initial period' indefinitely, or abolish the need for a referendum altogether. Finally, the Seanad, which had frustrated many of Mr. de Valera's legislative proposals, was abolished in 1936.

The effect of all these changes was that, by 1936, Dáil Eireann had assumed the character which the second Dáil had in 1921: it was the single-chamber parliament, unfettered by any limitation on its legislative capacity, of a State, republican in form, but – and this was the sole difference between 1921 and 1936 – associated with the States of the British Commonwealth for certain external purposes. By this time, the association could be claimed to be 'free' and not 'forced' as it had been at the inception of the Irish Free State in 1922.

The text of the Constitution had become a thing of shreds and patches, scarred by many changes and disfigured by Article 2A with its repressive powers.

It was clearly time for a new Constitution. Full national sovereignty had been attained. The only question which remained was whether such internal tranquillity had been established as to enable full civil liberty and the universal jurisdiction of the ordinary courts to be restored. The Government of the day apparently believed that it had, and Mr. de Valera now set about the preparation of a new fundamental Charter, a Constitution which he hoped, in his own words, would 'inspire as well as control, elicit loyalty as well as compel it. Every citizen should see in the basic public law of his country the sure safeguard of his individual rights as a human being, God-given rights which even the civil powers must not invade'.

The new Constitution, enacted by referendum held on July 1, 1937, is in many respects a remarkable document, especially in its assertion of a natural law philosophy which is Thomist and scholastic. Its carefully-phrased and elaborate provisions concerning personal and family rights and duties, education, private property and principles of social policy are derived from the Social Encyclicals, notably those of Pope Pius XI, *The Christian Education of Youth* (December, 1929), *Christian Marriage* (December, 1930)

170

and *Quadrigesimo Anno* (May, 1931). They follow, closely, in form and content, a synthesis of Catholic social principles known as The Social Code, prepared by the International Union of Social Studies, Malines, Belgium.

The Malines Union was founded in 1920 under the presidency of Cardinal Mercier to study social problems in the light of Catholic ethics. It has the rare distinction of having had its work acknowledged in a Papal Encyclical – *Quadrigesimo Anno*. The first edition of the Social Code appeared in 1927, the second in 1933.

The Constitution's Directive Principles of Social Policy, which are for the general guidance of the Oireachtas, and are not enforceable by the Courts, have provided a model for the Constitutions of India, Pakistan and Burma.

The treatment of religion in the Constitution is of particular interest. In acknowledging 'Our Divine Lord, Jesus Christ' it has impliedly accepted the truth of the Christian religion. It does not recognise the truth of any particular form of that religion. The Social Code, enumerating a number of acceptable methods for regulating the relations between Church and State, laid down as 'the best method' a regime in which 'the State recognises the rights which the Church derives from the higher importance of her spiritual end and itself publicly proclaims the Catholic Faith.' The Constitution, prudently, does not follow that line: it contents itself with the statement: 'The State recognises the special position of the Holy Catholic Apostolic and Roman Church as the guardian of the Faith possessed by the great majority of its citizens', proceeding then to 'recognise' the Church of Ireland, the Presbyterian Church in Ireland, the Methodist Church in Ireland, the Religious Society of Friends in Ireland, 'as well as the Jewish Congregations and the other religious denominations existing in Ireland at the date of the coming into operation of this Constitution'.

The Constitution of Burma adopted, with variations, the Irish model: 'The State recognises the special position of Buddhism as the faith professed by the great majority of the citizens of the Union. The State also recognises Islam, Christianity, Hinduism and Animism as some of the religions existing in the Union at the date of the coming into operation of this Constitution.'

The Irish provision has been compared with the terms of the Concordat of 1801 between Napoleon and Pope Pius VII, in which 'the Catholic, Apostolic and Roman religion' is recognised as 'the religion of the great majority of Frenchmen'. Mr de Valera has said, however, that any resemblance is purely coincidental. Of course, the circumstances were entirely different. The Concordat was putting an end to a period of war between Church and State, and reconstituting the Catholic Church in France; no Irish religious denomination had any cause of complaint against the laws of the land, nor was their status exalted by what was, in effect, an act of courtesy by the State, respecting and honouring religion.

The Constitution of 1937 was not merely a new legal enactment. The people gave to themselves not merely a new Constitution but a new 'sovereign, independent, democratic State.' Successive political leaders had brought the nation thus far, through the years of the great test, and if liberty had frequently been curtailed it could be pleaded that this had been directed against those political heretics, as Maritain described them, 'who threaten the unity of the community'. 'In a lay society of free men', he has written, in *Man and the State,* 'the heretic is one who rejects the common democratic beliefs and practices, one who takes a stand against freedom... or the moral power of the law'.

The year 1937 marked a new start, a fresh opportunity for the whole community. How it was availed of is a story for another day's telling.

CONCLUSION

T. Desmond Williams

Writers in the preceding fourteen papers have given their separate accounts of the years 1927 to 1937.

These dates were chosen principally for reasons of political history. They have more significance for the study of politics and parliament than for the history of ideas, economic or social developments. It was noteably a period of constitutional change, yet politics at any time is merely one aspect of a people's life. The less dramatic sides of economic and social movement, though harder to grasp and compress, may be more relevant. It is easier to write on politics, for here events are most conspicuous. Politics too is more concerned with individuals, less with the nameless crowd. Yet while politicians come and go, and parties rise and fall, the great problems of more impersonal character have a knack of remaining. So, despite the civil war, reconstruction in the twenties, and the political and constitutional revolutions inaugurated by de Valera in the thirties, divided Ireland, is still with us. Partition is no nearer a final solution. Immigration, until very recently, has been going on as in 1922, 1926 or 1937. And the restoration of the Irish language remains as scrappy as ever. On these three issues state policy has until recently scarcely advanced since the period under review. There was, of course, a considerable accumulation of capital during the war which followed fast after, and we are now enjoying some mirage of economic boom. During the years under discussion there was not much social change, but a good many of the social and economic phenomena we have now were partly founded then. At every point of time there must be change, but what is important to us scarcely seemed important then. Still the price of barley and the price of cattle did mean a lot to the last generation too.

In politics at any rate we still have many of the old

faces of those days. The great protagonists, de Valera and Cosgrave, are still talked about, though retired in very different ways from the arena. Other ageing political matadors, Lemass, Aiken and Ryan on the one side – Dillon, Costello and others – still influence many proceedings in the Dáil and Senate. The personal stability of the professional politician is one of the major factors in the history of modern Ireland. Very few have cracked up, compared to their counterparts of the thirties in Britain or the United States: family loyalties have reinforced the political structure all along. Constitutional revolution, combined with gradual economic change plus social stasis are obvious characteristics of those years, as of more recent ones.

And yet, in the tempestuous atmosphere of the Dáil in the late twenties and thirties, few on any side did in fact foresee the manner in which political passion would eventually subside and fierce controversy be resolved. Many were regarding their adversaries as murderers, and, in fact, calling them so. There were several political assassinations, – carried out by the I.R.A. – another institution which is still about, though barely and sporadically so. After 1932 the government behaved as if it saw fascists lurking behind corners occupied by members of the principal opposition party – Cumann na nGaedheal – its blueshirted allies and middle-class farmers. In contrast Dillon, Fitzgerald Kenny, Desmond Fitzgerald, Mulcahy and McGilligan denounced the personal dictatorship of de Valera. There was from 1932 onward an economic war between England and Ireland; the Senate was abolished – only to be restored later with attenuated powers – and those involved were constantly attributing the most sinister motives to their opponents. Crowds used hurley sticks in the old style against one another at political rallies. There was a growing stress on political affiliations, though it was very much there in the days of the Irish Parliamentary Party. Even on road work the political views of the ganger concerned had to be carefully considered. As the franchise broadened, local councils were sucked into political party divisions. Here as elsewhere the American rather than the British system extended. Though de Valera never secured or sought the powers of dictatorship, his personal mastery of the cabinet and Dáil was – when he really let himself go – without parallel. The tone and temper of parliamentary exchanges was often very bitter, but there was no breakdown in the machine of parliamentary procedure. Various scenes might be justly deplored; they could not nonetheless be compared with what was going on in Italian or German parliaments before the arrival of Mussolini or Hitler. The party system remained unimpaired. The basis for the existence of what virtually became a two-party arrangement was laid down by a crucial decision taken in 1927 – to admit Fianna Fáil into the Dáil on the basis of the declaration concerning the oath of allegiance as an 'empty formula'. This was a great turning point in the history of parliamentary government in Ireland.

In that parliamentary history there were other dangerous moments, but these came from without, not from within Leinster House. What we do not know is the extent to which William T. Cosgrave knew he was making a fundamental decision, carrying with it the ultimate fall of his own government and the tremendous advantage to constitutional politics of channelling the rising tide of republicanism to the system of representative democracy. When de Valera came into power five years later, his success in subduing the I.R.A. extremists to his left, and in outmanoeuvring or outwitting the Blueshirts also helped to fortify the same system. And then, too, despite public safety acts, the suspension of *habeas corpus,* and the establishment of military tribunals especially in 1931, there never was the slightest attempt to interfere with the liberty of the press. The Irish Independent could, and did say what it liked about de Valera throughout; the Irish Press, as a pro-government paper after 1932 gave the Fianna Fáil version of contemporary history; and the Irish Times, under the editorship of Smylie, annoyed everyone from time to time, whilst pleasing many readers by its apparent independence. The followers of the Workers' Republic, or of the simple Republic, had their own organs of print. The rule of law was fundamentally maintained, both by Cosgrave and de Valera. Each indeed made use of emergency legislation, involving the partial suspension of that rule, but their suspensions were carefully limited. The military courts were fair and from time to time rejected the demands of the state prosecutor. The intellectual standards of the judiciary may have varied, but the judges respected themselves and were respected by the state. On the main issues of a liberal and democratic concept of society there was a remarkable consensus of opinion between the revolutionary constitutionalist, de Valera and the more prosaic constitutionalist Cosgrave. Men fought and distrusted one another, but generally within the rules of the parliamentary club, excepting the outsiders; the I.R.A. and the admirers of the Soviet Union. As for General O'Duffy and his Blueshirts, they never really knew what they wanted.

The ideological presuppositions of Irish society based on the constitutions of 1922 and 1937 were not – for any student of government and politics – so dissimilar. The law, in historical origins, was English; the principle of a written constitution was American; the moral and religious content was Christian. Constitutions, of course, are very often what the lawyers and politicians make them, but all sections of Irish society were then agreed upon the fundamental ends of government. Even if people lived in protracted struggle, they met at similar funerals. The Irish in the south were predominantly Catholic; unlike other states, religious prejudice did not degenerate into religious struggles. Yet in Dublin the leading bankers and insurance brokers were still Protestant. The percentage of Protestants and masons in medicine and law also was remarkably high – far beyond their percentage in the population as a whole. The governments of Cumann na nGaedheal and Fianna Fáil left them alone. And politics was run in '22 in '27 and in '37 by the Catholics who controlled a power which they did not abuse. Protestants in public life remained odd fish. De Valera was obviously independent regarding the role of the Irish Catholic Church in politics. He participated in the undenominational political tradition of republicanism – more so probably than Cumann na nGaedheal. This hardly touched domestic issues between

176

'32 and '37. A number of his followers were Catholics, who had ceased to be churchgoers – for a time – on account of excommunications during the civil war. Others were more instinctively anticlerical, not only on account of the civil war, but also by way of intellectual affiliations with Tone, the Fenians and secret societies. Cumann na nGaedheal were more in the tradition of the constitutional wing of Irish politics – of John Dillon, Tim Healy and John Redmond, (also of the tradition of the Ancient Order of Hibernians). De Valera on one occasion made sure that a few of his colleagues would resign from the Knights of St. Columbanus, an organisation not entirely unfamiliar (then or now) with the activities of the A.O.H. But then again, he as Taoiseach in 1936 and 1937 drafted certain articles of the constitution in close collaboration with the ecclesiastic who subsequently became Archbishop of Dublin. Cosgrave was accused in the 1932 election of collaboration with free-masons in a somewhat silly, though presumably effective electioneering pamphlet, issued under the auspices of Sean MacEntee. Fianna Fáil therefore to the annoyance of its parliamentary opposition, appeared to have it both ways. But in 1932 as well, Messrs Arthur Guinness and co in particular, and John Jameson and co, and Trinity College were very worried about the possible implications of the de Valera revolution – not so much on account of their Protestant inheritance, more because of their old connections with the Ascendancy and their economic contacts with England. These timidities proved to be unfounded. There was to be no expropriation; they could remain in their Irish Club.

It was in the field of foreign affairs that de Valera's independence from denominationalist politics shone out more clearly. In public controversy over the League of Nations, the policy of sanctions against Italy during the Abyssinian crisis, and of non-intervention throughout the Spanish civil war, the Taoiseach differed most markedly in nuance and direction from the attitudes of Cumann na nGaedheal, which by now had changed its name to Fine Gael. Pius XII supported fascist Italy in Abyssinia. De Valera opposed it. O'Duffy, now in lonely isolation, had organised an Irish brigade to go to Spain in aid of General Franco. And a nationalist government was installed in 1936 at Burgos. Collections were held outside church gates in defence of the Irish Brigade fighting for the so-called Christian crusade of Franco against communism. De Valera supported the policy of non-intervention and refused to recognise Franco's nationalist regime, despite repeated demands from Cosgrave and Fine Gael that he should do so straight away. Instead he supported the policies advocated at Geneva by Britain and France (and 49 other states). Here he did take the risk of being denounced in some quarters as an international opponent of Catholic Spain and Catholic Italy

By republicans, by liberals and by the Irish Times he was defended as supporting democracy and opposing fascism on the international scene. He had appeared first on that scene in 1932 – as president of the council, and on one notable occasion had vehemently defended the rights of small states. His political opponents played this up as a smart trick. De Valera, professedly the arch-nationalist in home politics, was now playing the internationalist abroad. Partly through this role at Geneva, he managed to gain a fair amount of international standing for his name and his country. Before the last world war, he had achieved a favoured name for himself with an unusual combination of international politicians: and this position he was to exploit subsequently – with Genevan 'internationalists', the international liberal press, Adolf Hitler and Neville Chamberlain. This assisted his later discussions with German legation diplomats in Dublin. Far more it assisted his diplomatic negotiations with British civil servants and the British prime minister in the Spring of 1938.

Though there was much argument in the Dáil, foreign affairs were not of major interest to the Irish public. Anyhow after 1936 parliamentary debates were far more prosaic, (and to that extent 'normal'). More serious and less passionate discussion went on about industrial and agricultural policies. The Cosgrave administration had introduced some elements of native industrial development: the Shannon scheme being the most outstanding.

The Sugar co. was another of their enterprises – and, in the first 'hundred days' of de Valera's regime, these were rashly dismissed by one prominent minister as 'white elephants'. On the industrial side, Lemass as soon as he entered office began his industrial revolution in 1932. As Minister for Industry and Commerce, he was the most vigorous, aggressive and original protegé of the leader. Even in 1932 if not in 1927 he was apparently being groomed for the succession. In debates his contributions were harsh, practical and efficient; but at that stage they revealed a conventional mind. Agriculture was more poorly handled, this being the weakest area in which a government involved in economic war did engage in cogent argument. There are many arguments for and against any policy of self-sufficiency. Such validity as they may have depends on the particular circumstances of the time during which they are advocated – more than on any reasons offered in public controversy. Arthur Griffith as a prophet had inaugurated and Alfred Rahilly as an academic continued the abstract case for self-sufficiency.

De Valera from the beginning had a philosophy of politics partly based on the preservation of the small farmer and the social unit centred around him. He had grown up in this world alongside the landless labourer. As he once put it on a celebrated occasion: he had only to look into his own heart to know what they, the Irish people were thinking. This type of society was essentially a conservative one. It did not understand or accept the maximisation of capital wealth as a principal object to state policy. The world of an t'Athair Peader O'Laoghaire and industrial capitalism were far apart. That conservative political policy admitted a profit motive, but did not put too great a price on it. No man, de Valera once indicated, was worth more than £1,000 a year: and he had even talked of substituting ale and milk for tea and other imported groceries. But you could not get very far ahead in an nationalist industrial revolution without a strong concern for profits, with a system basically devoted to free enterprise. Lemass was the most urban and economically sophisticated of the Fianna Fáil ministers. De Valera appeared not to want to understand fully all the implications of industrialisation. Despite their radical differences over constitutional issues of oath and commonwealth, Dillon and de Valera seemed in 1937 more identified with a rural than with an urban civilisation – though they represented a different strata of that community here. But the Taoiseach was not an ideologue – rather a politician, par excellence, skilled in the game of maintaining political power; and his political philosophy was to be enshrined in the 1937 constitution. So Lemass had his way on the industrial front, as far as he could go.

The policy of home-grown wheat expressed more clearly the political philosophy of De Valera and Aiken, both being closely allied also in advocating the restoration of the Irish language as a spoken tongue. The wheat policy was to pay dividends during the war. It played an important part in maintaining neutrality, but it had not been introduced on that account. It was around agriculture rather than industrialisation that the most passionate controversies sprang up. The campaign for home-grown wheat and against grass and cattle after 1932 became gradually linked with the constitutional disagreement over the payment of land annuities to the British government. There was no necessary connection, but it so happened. Many of the richer middle class farmers were ruined by consequence of the economic war. The refusal of some of them to pay rates became part of Blueshirt policy. Attempts were made to stop auctions of goods seized for non-payment of rates and the government had strong recourse to the dubious policy of employing buyers under police protection; and military tribunals were quite frequently also called in to try some of the defaulters. The parliamentary opposition took care to dissociate itself publicly from any resistance to the normal processes of law, but it sympathised with what it considered the victimisation of Fianna Fáil policy. There was very little class war in the Ireland of the time, but class tensions between richer and poorer members of the farming community often surfaced. Their significance could be much exaggerated, though disparities of wealth in the countryside certainly gave rise to social distrust, if not hatred. These were not, however, in any way to be compared with the old conflict between Anglo-Irish landlords and land leaguers. Then there was a real social revolution, worthy of note in the textbooks of economic history. Meanwhile the Land Commission functioned smoothly enough and some landless men got land. Lemass's industrial meanwhile revolution remained very far from completion on the one hand; and in agriculture the atmosphere stayed depressed and strained until the ending of the economic war between Ireland and Britain in 1938 and the outbreak of the second world war in 1939.

There were some major blunders in the conduct of this economic and social policy. These led to constant altercations between the front and back benchers in the Dáil. The attempt to provide free beef, the wholesale slaughter of calves and the Roscrea meat factory were discussed again and again in terms of political corruption. All revolutions produce situations of this kind. The prospect of great and sudden changes shows up ambition and greed. There will be new jobs for the new boys, new contracts going. It is easier as always for the comfortable classes to avoid the more conspicuous forms of jobbery. But there was an invisible trade union of the respectable and professional classes. And as the revolutionary parties settle down, they too become respectable. Old enmities and passions were submerged and the courtesies of political and social life reappeared. Much of the animosity between the two main parties of the civil war period still remained at the close of these years, but there had been no violent social changes. The civil service, the army and the police were fundamentally unaltered. The venture of the Broy harriers – a new kind of special political police – came to nothing. Whatever their purpose, they proved unneeded and were subsequently dissolved. The substance of the state had not been radically transformed.

There were, of course, new faces and some new experiments in government. The state-assisted companies were beginning. Nearly all of them were sharply criticised by the opposition at the start. Nothing good could come out of de Valera's Ireland. But on the whole the companies stood the test of time, responding well later to the challenge of war and further economic expansion. The traditional Irish world of economists and bankers was more sceptical of the new policies of state participation in industry than were some overseas economists – notably John Maynard Keynes. Aer Lingus was in the planning stage only. Transport was then in its usual muddle. The turf board was well on its way towards vigorous expansion and there was no tourism as we now know it. New skills were being acquired, which could, however, be only tested convincingly during and after the second world war.

Each generation has its own problems, failures and successes in handling them. What is the historical setting of this whole period? It was the age of the founding of a new state. Like many states, it had a very shaky start with a civil war. Cosgrave's government in its second stage pursued a policy of consolidation between 1927 and 1932. It had solved the military problems posed by the civil war. It did not succeed in resolving the political or social ones. It performed a remarkable task in building up the foundations of the Free State of 1922 and had successfully achieved a British legal system modified to suit Irish conditions, a parliamentary system and a bureaucracy. Cosgrave coped reasonalby well with the economic stresses of a very dangerous world. We may think badly of our own opponents in our own political framework at any time. It is sometimes salutory and not uninspiring to look around and see how others are doing in other worlds. By that test the Ireland of '27 to '37 does not come off too badly – certainly in comparison with far greater powers. The country lived to some extent upon capital derived from its past. It certainly did not exhaust that capital materially or culturally. People began to get over the civil war by 1936 – though the politicians were loth to let them forget it. It may still remain a personal issue among some politicians, but memories are long in other countries too.

How far did that Ireland add to the capital inherited? This is always a very difficult question to answer – especially where it relates to the imponderables of economics, social advance, religion and culture. There were moments when Irish society gave an appearance of some disintegration – in 1927, 1931, 1934 and 1935. Government and opposition sometimes appeared to think so. But by 1937 those danger spots had gone – even though few contemporaries could appreciate it. The universal acceptance of the constitution introduced towards the end of 1937 and the unqualified recognition of de Valera's modified 'new political order' closed the era of political revolution – stretching from 1916 to 1937.

New ages must carry their inheritance; the ideology of 1916 and the historical myths of Irish nationalists were to influence and distort political developments for some time to come, but this did not arise out of any serious defects in constitutional arrangements. The I.R.A. managed to survive aggressively but ineffectively long after 1937. This was more a fault in the educational system than in anything else. Here the schools, the universities and the Department of Education must bear their share of responsibility – with special reference to the teaching of history. The older versions of history were (as they still are) essentially political. It is not so much the fact of continuing partition that explained (and still explains) the republican irreconcilables as the type of history taught about partition and its long-term historical origins. A sense of unnecessary nationalist grievance about the Irish past added to discontent about the present. Here there was really no progress at all. This naturally affected the cultural contributions of those years. The intellectuals were difficult to satisfy. Hence a good deal of empty whining and invective. Some divine discontentment is desirable; much of the Irish was sour. Yet in ordinary daily life the people then were much better off than we tend to think. In the practical business of surviving, in developing new communities abroad, in assisting the sick and the poor, also in avoiding extreme disparities in social relationships, that generation did not do too badly. It was certainly a good deal less spoilt than the present one.

If you would like to receive our
complete catalogue send your name
and address to
THE MERCIER PRESS
4 Bridge Street, Cork
Ireland

First published in the Netherlands and printed by Bosch, Utrecht